Advance Praise for
So You've Been Sent to Diversity Training

"You should read Chadwick Moore, truly a gifted writer."

-Tucker Carlson, Fox News host

"In the leftist madness all around us, voices of sanity are rare. Fortunately, we have Chadwick Moore, who delivers a brilliantly crafted and ruthless takedown of the petty, sour little despots ruining America—and does it with a wicked sense of humor that will have you laughing out loud from page one. So You've Been Sent to Diversity Training blows the lid off the DEI insanity, relentlessly mocks its practitioners, and fortifies you for the battle against it. An important, hilarious, and cool read."

–Monica Crowley, Ph.D., media personality, bestselling author, and host of the Monica Crowley Podcast

"Chadwick Moore's hilarious, insightful first book—So You've Been Sent to Diversity Training—is a must read for anyone who wants to take their country back from the Marxist mob. Moore brings together whistleblowers from all walks of life who speak out about the insane and often hateful DEI instruction they're forced to endure just to keep their jobs. A wokeness pandemic has been spreading through America—and Chadwick's book is a vaccine that actually works."

–Buck Sexton, conservative commentator and co-host of the Clay Travis and Buck Sexton Show

"A menace to the gay community and mankind in general."

–Someone on Twitter

SO YOU'VE BEEN SENT TO DIVERSITY TRAINING

SMILING THROUGH
THE **DEI APOCALYPSE**

Chadwick Moore

BOMBARDIER
BOOKS

Published by Bombardier Books
An Imprint of Post Hill Press
ISBN: 978-1-63758-135-3
ISBN (eBook): 978-1-63758-136-0

So You've Been Sent to Diversity Training:
Smiling Through the DEI Apocalypse
© 2022 by Chadwick Moore
All Rights Reserved

Cover photo by Rachel Herman-Gabrielli

Cover Design by Tiffani Shea

Interior Design by Yoni Limor

Post Hill Press
New York • Nashville
posthillpress.com

Published in the United States of America
1 2 3 4 5 6 7 8 9 10

For my dad,
Who always taught me to call out the bullshit.

Contents

Chapter One

To Browbeat and Belittle:
The NYPD Goes to Gay Education Camp

'm rushing through the halls of a building that looks like
the set of a new *Star Trek* movie. Young cadets meander
silently two by two dressed in tidy, gray uniforms that
blend in with imposing gunmetal columns, the geometric
light fixtures, and perforated steel railings. It's an austere,
otherworldly setting for New York's $950 million
Police Academy, in College Point, Queens, a sprawling,
thirty-two acre, 750,000-square-foot complex completed
one year earlier. It's a spring afternoon in 2015, and I'm
about to have my first experience with diversity and inclusion training.

I'm here on assignment for a gay magazine where I
worked at the time. In the classroom a stout, cartoonish
lesbian—built like a meatball—draws a stick figure on a
dry-erase board. She's a former patrol officer in the 34th
Precinct, just north of Harlem, and the stick figure has
broad shoulders, a cinched waist, two dots for eyes, a
crude smile, and a faux-hawk hairdo. The class votes to
name him Caleb.

"What's Caleb carrying with him?" the officer asks the
room of about seventy young, mostly male, cadets.

"A messenger bag," someone calls out. She draws a messenger bag.

"What kind of shoes is he wearing?"

"Boat shoes," another calls out.

"Where does Caleb live?"

"Chelsea," says one cadet.

"Williamsburg," says another. The class laughs. She writes "Williamsburg" on the board.

"What does our stereotypical gay guy do for work?" the officer asks.

"He's got money," calls out one cadet.

"Hairdresser," says another.

"Finance."

They take a vote. Caleb works in finance.

"Where do we get these ideas about Caleb?" the officer asks. A murmur percolates: the streets, media, advertising.

"Do you know what the term 'heterosexist' means?" she asks. "What about the term 'homophobic'?"

The two-hour course, titled "LGBT-Sensitivity Training," is required for students preparing to enter New York City's nearly thirty-five-thousand–member police force, where roughly fifteen hundred cadets graduate annually. I've been sent here to report on the progress the NYPD is making to tackle its homophobia problem. Except I don't see a homophobia problem, never have, and especially not among the future officers gathered here today.

A leggy brunette in a pencil skirt then addresses the class. Officer Brooke Bukowski of the 70th Precinct reveals herself to be transgender and the cadets straighten in their seats. "You can ask me anything you want," Bukowski tells the class, and a dozen hands shoot into the air.

"But don't ask me about my genitals," she scolds. She's done this before, apparently. The hands slink back down. Honestly, what else would you really want to know?

An egghead who'd been taking notes raises his hand. "If there's a dead body and they can't tell you their preferred name and gender, but their license says male, what do you do?" he asks.

"As a cop you have to put what it legally says on the paperwork, but you're not writing the obituary, so don't worry," Bukowski says.

The atmosphere is light and spirited, like a field trip, and participants are encouraged to unbutton their collars, kick back, and relax. Way back in 1978 New York City mayor Ed Koch signed an executive order banning discrimination based on sexual orientation in all city agencies. As I listened to the gay cop trainers prattle on, I remembered being in Greenwich Village outside the iconic Stonewall Inn the night in June 2011, where four years earlier, the New York State legislature had just legalized gay marriage. Hundreds showed up for a spontaneous celebration. At a moment's notice the NYPD had set up barricades to allow revelers to carry on well into the night. Cops were high fiving the crowd, telling them "Congratulations!" and turning a blind eye to celebrants binging on booze and marijuana in the streets. It was a heartwarming scene.

The Stonewall Inn, now a national historic landmark, was the site of the three-day uprising in June of 1969 that sparked the modern gay rights movement. It's why there's a Pride month in June and a reminder that those tacky and sex-charged, corporate-sponsored Pride parades we see today were once political marches for equal rights held each year on the anniversary of the Stonewall rebellion. Although the legend of Stonewall has been perverted in recent years by the fever dreams of activists, falsely claiming the whole thing was started by "trans women of color"(it wasn't, none were there, the crowd was almost entirely white, gay men and the term "transgender" didn't exist yet), a clash between police officers and gay men instigated the weekend-long act of civil disobedience. Here we'd come full circle in a way those old queens from the Stonewall days could have never imagined.

And yet today in the eyes of Big Diversity, the NYPD seemed to have a profound masculinity problem. "Do you agree that lesbians have it easier on the force than gay men?" a forty-six-year-old gay male cop asked the cadets in a challenging way that afternoon. "What do we do to a lesbian on the job? We make her into one of the guys, take her to the strip club. The gay guy, what do we do with him? We feminize him, make him weaker, bitchy, catty. Is he going to be one of the guys?" he asks.

No, the cadets groan.

"Half of gays and lesbians in New York City don't report to the police because they expect that the police department is homophobic and that we don't care. They're afraid you're going to make fun of them," he says.

Is that the NYPD's fault, I wondered? Sure, some cops might make fun of them—gay people tend to be ridiculous—but not to their faces. Most of the gay men I knew who didn't call the police perhaps when they should have all had the same story: They got drunk, or high, and brought home a stranger who then made off with their iPhone or wallet. I'd be lying if I said that had never happened to me, and countless friends, who woke up ashamed of their irresponsible behavior and too embarrassed to file a police report the next day.

Was this really a result of systemic homophobia? You'd be hard pressed to find many out-and-proud New York homosexuals—and most New York gays are insufferably out and proud—who'd hesitate to call the police, the newspapers, or set up a GoFundMe if they felt they'd been targeted for a crime specifically because of their sexuality rather than questionable decisions found at the bottom of bottles.

Take, for example, the Cinco de Mayo Dallas BBQ antigay hate crime of 2015. A young, white gay couple—the type usually called "twinks" in the tribal vernacular—was leaving the Dallas BBQ restaurant on the corner of

Eighth Avenue and 23rd Street in Chelsea, Manhattan's signature gay neighborhood, around 11 p.m., when on his way out, one of the twinks accidently knocked over a drink.

"A table near us audibly started making pretty gross comments about the two of us like, 'white faggots, spilling drinks,'" the man told a video reporter for the website DNAinfo. "I don't let anyone talk to me like that. I went over there and asked, 'What did you say about us?'"

A confrontation ensued, resulting in a hulking, six-foot-six guy cracking a wooden chair over the man's head. The next day, the couple were on the news and the city was agog. How could this happen, here of all places?

"The fact that this attack took place in the neighborhood of Chelsea, a place known around the world for its acceptance of all people, is particularly outrageous," Chris Johnson, the gay city councilman for Chelsea, fulminated at the time.

A manhunt ensued and the NYPD's Hate Crimes Task Force got involved. Dallas BBQ commissioned an elaborate sign and posted it in their window, denouncing "hateful behavior" and telling passersby that "Dallas BBQ celebrates a diverse clientele at all our locations."

Two weeks later, the suspect was identified as forty-two-year-old Bronx resident Bayna-Lekheim El-Amin. By that time, the victim, Jonathan Snipes, thirty-three, admitted to instigating the altercation by hitting El-Amin first with his "light purse" before the incident became an all-out brawl. Then we learned that El-Amin was also gay. The hate crime charges, and the media hype, disappeared. The "white" part of his "white faggot" remark didn't seem to meet the hate crime criteria.

After El-Amin's guilty verdict, gay rights groups penned a letter to the judge pleading for leniency.

"It is clear that race was the underlying issue that led to the altercation. It is common knowledge that racism within the gay community is a serious problem. It is common for white gay men to act with hostility toward men of color in gay establishments. It is common for gay men of color to experience racist attitudes and behavior from white gay men. The reporting in the mainstream and gay press about this incident echoed the racism that gay men of color experience at gay bars and elsewhere," the group wrote. El-Amin was sentenced to nine years.

Like many pieces I wrote at that time, I felt pressure to tow a certain party line, in this case anticop, when covering their diversity-training curriculum. When the story went to print, even the headline, which another editor wrote, was backhanded. "Can you teach sensitivity?" it asked.

But I couldn't bring myself to besmirch the cops. Everyone I encountered was so likable. They were intelligent, well-meaning, self-aware, and socially percipient, despite not going to Harvard or Berkeley. They were having fun and seemed genuinely open to new perspectives. I thought, this is the real NYPD, not the image painted by liberal class prejudices noisily informing gay and minority perspectives. And while any member of the liberal Soylent-sipping nobility who observed that course may have scoffed or pearl-clutched at the cadets' obtuseness on certain aspects of the LGBT lifestyle, their ignorance was never tinged with malice. If anything, it came off as suitably charming.

Even Snipes, the purse-wielding Dallas BBQ victim, commended the NYPD, writing on Facebook, "We live in the finest city in the world and have the VERY BEST police officers to match! I am humbled and immensely thankful for their help. Even in the midst of turmoil we feel so blessed to have been shown such compassion."

By this time I was growing skeptical of the media business, and it came to a head the following year. After the 2016 election, the biggest story I saw around me was not only the failure of my colleagues to see what was really going on in politics, but every journalist's blind allegiance to a narrative that served the Democratic Party.

I was very naïve in early 2017. That's the year I got canceled before the term "cancel culture" existed. I looked around for weeks on social media and saw my colleagues in emotional free-fall over the election of Donald Trump to the presidency. According to the Twitter posts from many journalists I knew, the sky was on fire; the world was ending; Klansmen were marching into the White House. It was all hands on deck to "resist!"

Resist what? I wondered. This was highly unprofessional behavior.

On Inauguration Day, I watched tens of thousands of radicals parading around Washington, D.C., as part of what they branded the "Women's March," protesting the free and fair election of our new president and getting cheered on by intellectually broken journalists across the country. If thousands of journalists, including all my bosses, were allowed to speak their minds so freely about politics, I assumed it would be O.K. if I had my say, too. With the help of Michael Kaplan at the *New York Post*, I penned a column with the headline, "I'm a gay New Yorker, and I'm coming out conservative."

"And I began to realize that maybe my opinions just didn't fit in with the liberal status quo, which seems to mean that you must absolutely hate Trump, his supporters, and everything they believe. If you dare not to protest or boycott Trump, you are a traitor," I said in the column.

"If you dare to question liberal stances or make an effort toward understanding why conservatives think the way they do, you are a traitor. It can seem like liberals are actually against free speech if it fails to conform with the way they think. And I don't want to be a part of that club anymore."

I didn't think of myself as a whistleblower. I wasn't trying to throw a bomb and never would have participated in the piece had everyone else around me not been so preoccupied with announcing their own politics. I did it for peace of mind. I wanted anyone who was listening to know: Just because I'm gay, live in New York, and work in media, I am not like these people. They don't speak for me, and I don't want to be associated with them.

I thought it was rather innocent. This was America, after all. Don't we have the right to speak our minds and disagree?

Apparently not. The story went viral and I got fired. At that week's frosty editorial meeting for the gay magazine where I worked, no one addressed me. Later that night, the editor-in-chief called to tell me I was being let go. He was frazzled. A month earlier, over coffee, discussing nothing related to politics—I was concerned about recent downsizing—he hugged me when we left and told me not to worry. "As long as I'm running this magazine, you'll always have a job here," he said. He always seemed to have my back. He appreciated my contrarian perspective and taste for oddball stories. I was the only writer at the magazine who wasn't a wacky social justice warrior, a pathetic celebrity-chaser, or a desperate fashion world neophyte. Now word came from above to get rid of me and I don't think he was pleased about it.

Yet, on Twitter in the weeks leading up, this editor was one of the most Trump-deranged of them all. How much of that was an act, I wondered, plunging into the center of the blood-orgy to broadcast one's allegiance to power? For every dissident choosing silence, as I once did, you can bet there's another baying support in consternation. Like North Koreans at a dictator's funeral, you might feel a muzzle in your back if you're too quiet.

What I also didn't realize at the time I wrote about sensitivity training at the NYPD is that what had seemed like a one-off lecture preparing the nation's largest police force to interact with homosexuals was, in fact, another micron in an enterprise that had been gaining scope and influence for decades.

What started as a fringe consulting enterprise on the margins of business and government has become institutionalized and well-nigh inescapable in the workplace. Teaching sensitivity to people in uniform who engage with the public morphed into an industry of hocus pocus that does not only include "training" around correct thought about LGBTs, but about race, gender, and other issues. Diversity training got 'roided up and is unmistakably everywhere: from retail workers, to coal miners, to bank CEOs. Your job has probably required you to sit through at least one tedious harangue by a stranger who explains, in the most condescending and frequently insulting way, everything you've already picked up on your own merely by living in a diverse society filled with many different types of people.

The golden rule, treat others as you'd like to be treated, which used to serve us well, has gone completely out the door. In the seven years that followed that class, discussions of race, gender, and sexuality have grown increasingly strident in media and political messaging. In the summer of 2020, following the death of George Floyd, race hysteria came to dominate nearly every aspect of American life. Workplaces scrambled to address the news headlines, despite few asking them to do so, and employees noticed that the innocuous bromides about tolerance and acceptance to which they'd become accustomed took a sharply radical turn.

For the NYPD, the countless hours spent educating tens of thousands of officers on LGBT sensitivity were all for nothing. The police, in the eyes of powerful activists, were now a greater threat than ever, no matter the amount of penance, goodwill, or department-wide indoctrination. In May 2021, Heritage of Pride, the organization that runs New York City's LGBT Pride festivities—by far the largest in the country, possibly the world—banned police officers from marching in uniform until at least the year 2025, when the organization said the policy would be reviewed again. This included gay cops, who'd marched alongside other groups in the annual Pride parade for four decades. Police officers, however, would still be required to provide security for the event.

"The sense of safety that law enforcement is meant to provide can instead be threatening, and at times dangerous, to those in our community who are most often targeted with excessive force and/or without reason," the organizers said in a press release. "NYC Pride is unwilling to contribute in any way to creating an atmosphere of fear or harm for members of the community." The Gay Officers Action League, the group of cops that conducts LGBT trainings for the force, responded, saying they were disheartened and the "abrupt about-face in order to placate some of the activists in our community is shameful."

None of this was about diversity. Employers everywhere were suddenly preaching a wicked and immoral philosophy called critical race theory (CRT for short), the idea that the law and legal institutions are inherently racist and that race itself, rather than being rooted in biology, is a social construct used by white people to further the economic and political interests of whites at the expense of other races. CRT argues that poverty and criminality in many minority communities is the intended result of white people who are attempting to create legal and economic divisions between the races to advance white interests in economics and politics. It's a conspiracy theory, perhaps the most pervasive, destructive, and legitimized one in history. As with all conspiracy theories, proselytes use highly skewed data alongside anecdotal evidence to reinforce their deeply held fictions.

Meanwhile anyone who complained or objected was gaslit with a sinister argument that any resistance to the new ideological program is merely an expression of "white fragility." In this way all objections were dismissed and dissenting individuals shamed or coerced into silence. As a result, the vast majority of those who have been subjected to these trainings have gone along meekly to avoid being humiliated, disciplined, or fired.

Nevertheless, a growing number of people have felt driven to sound the alarm. In New Mexico, for instance, in the summer of 2020 a young engineer named Casey Peterson at the Sandia National Laboratories, one of three National Nuclear Security Administration research and development laboratories in the United States, became disturbed by what he saw going on. He works in a federally funded nuclear lab pivotal to national security interests, and the government was using the taxpayers' money to tell white male employees they're evil and everyone else that they're hopeless victims of a system designed to exterminate them.

"Despite my extensive efforts to point out the blatant lies and deep immorality of these resources and classes, no changes were made. I offered to host a class correcting the record. I was told that the company is not hosting a forum for debate and to keep my opinions at home and to get back to work. I was told by the senior manager of HR that, 'it is not our job to fact check the materials for accuracy,'" Peterson says in a lecture uploaded to YouTube about his experience with critical race theory training on the job.

"The way systemic racism and white privilege are represented and taught today are, at a minimum, contro-versial and vastly overblown. It does not belong in the workplace. Much of the mainstream claims and data are outright false. Racism is not a public health crisis and systemic racism is not a major problem," he says.

"What are these claims? America is chronically, systemically racist. Racism is a public health crisis. Silence is compliance, or even silence is violence. You must be an activist. This is a 'you're with us or against us' type of thinking and is directly in opposition to dialogue and diversity of thinking. Color blindness is racist. And the validity of your ideas is dependent upon the color of your skin. Many of these materials seem to be dedicated to convincing you that even you are unconsciously racist."

Peterson worked for five years as an electrical engineer at the Sandia labs. Before that he was an infantryman in the U.S. Army. A document posted to an internal website for lab employees titled "75 Things White People Could Do for Racial Justice" suggested employees donate to highly controversial, politically charged groups such as Black Lives Matter and the Southern Poverty Law Center. It labeled *Breitbart News* "white supremacist media" and claimed Fox News "radicalized" people.

Peterson combed through a reading list of twenty titles provided to employees on how to be an "antiracist." "Antiracism," a newfangled preoccupation of critical race theorists, entered the mainstream zeitgeist around the Floyd era. It holds that simply not being racist isn't enough; one must actively seek out and confront racism—at work, at the bus stop, within your family, at home lurking under the bed, or hiding in your kids' cereal. Racism exists everywhere and, as such, must be actively exposed and eliminated.

The books Peterson's job recommended included *White Fragility*, *White Rage*, *Me and White Supremacy*, *How to be an Anti-Racist*, and *Why I'm No Longer Talking to White People*. He found thirteen of the twenty books discussed critical race theory positively, while the other seven did not mention it. Twelve out of twenty expressed deep hatred for President Donald Trump, twelve were negative about former President Ronald Reagan, ten mentioned the Bush family negatively, and twelve were positive about former President Barack Obama. Sixteen out of twenty were antipolice.

Peterson's story caught the eye of Fox News host Tucker Carlson. After Carlson covered Peterson's account, the White House took note. All of this was, embarrassingly, occurring in a government workplace under President Trump's watch. The report joined other stories about federal agencies peddling similar ideologies. NASA had announced that in order to stamp out "systemic discrimination and inequality," it would rename the "Eskimo Nebula" and "Siamese Twins Galaxy." The National Museum for African American History and Culture, an institution created by the federal government, received widespread backlash that summer for publishing a graphic that linked things like "rugged individualism," the nuclear family, being on-time, and "decision-making" to whiteness. After Peterson's story got out, Republican Senator Josh Hawley of Missouri sent a letter to the Department of Energy demanding to know why Sandia labs was requiring its white male employees attend something called a "White Men's Caucus on Eliminating Racism, Sexism, and Homophobia in Organizations."

President Trump said his administration wouldn't allow "race or sex stereotyping or scapegoating in the federal workplace" or permit federal contractors to "inculcate such views in their employees." In late September, President Trump signed an executive order barring federal funds from any contractors who conduct critical race theory training for their employees. He called the trainings part of a "destructive ideology" that is "grounded in misrepresentations of our country's history and its role in the world."

"This ideology is rooted in the pernicious and false belief that America is an irredeemably racist and sexist country. That some people, simply on account of their race or sex, are oppressors; and that racial and sexual identities are more important than our common status as human beings and Americans."

"Such ideas may be fashionable in the academy, but they have no place in programs and activities supported by federal taxpayer dollars," President Trump said. "Research also suggests that blame-focused diversity training reinforces biases and decreases opportunities for minorities."

The executive order had no lasting impact. Biden was declared the winner of the 2020 election and on Inauguration Day signed his own executive order reversing Trump's policy on critical race theory training for federal workers and contractors.

"In the weeks ahead, I will be reaffirming the federal government's commitment to diversity, equity and inclusion and accessibility, building on the work we started in the Obama-Biden administration. That's why I'm rescinding the previous administration's harmful ban on diversity and sensitivity training," Biden said the day before signing the order. "Unity and healing must begin with understanding and truth, not ignorance and lies."

Policing had become the hottest topic in critical race theory trainings. In the YouTube lecture Peterson describes another panel hosted by his company's HR department titled "The Black Community and Law Enforcement." Attendees were shown two videos, both produced by left-wing media organizations, *Vox* and NPR. One, focused on the history of police brutality against blacks, jumped nearly one hundred years from the Ku Klux Klan to present day, ignoring all the social change that occurred in the decades between, Peterson says. The other relied heavily on statistics that did not consider population benchmarks, a tactic critical race theorists depend upon to advance their ideology.

Following the video, the all-black panel shared personal stories about dealing with police. "We know that police are dangerous to the black community," one said.

"What they're policing is the normalcy of white supremacy and these societal norms and behaviors that we have determined are acceptable by a certain group of people. And if someone else who doesn't look like that certain group of people are [sic] seen exercising those same privileges, then there is concern all of a sudden, because it's not what they see as the social and societal norm," Peterson reported another said.

"Throwing fuel on a fire that is unjustly burning is profoundly depraved. Numerous trainings and materials from our HR Department discussed how we teach our white and black children about policing in America and how to interact with police in America. If we, as a nation, are teaching our black children critical race theory then they are going to go into every police interaction with some combination of fear, anger, and nervousness. This is not making them or the officers safer. This rhetoric needs to stop," Peterson says in the video.

Despite pervasive public opinion believing otherwise, none of the hysteria surrounding law enforcement and racial minorities is remotely based on fact. On the contrary, when you dive into the data, it's quite impressive that more black men aren't killed by police officers each year.

According to the Department of Justice, for example, about 61.5 million Americans aged sixteen or older had at least one contact with police in 2018. Whites were significantly more likely than blacks or Hispanics to experience police contact. Twenty-six percent of the white population had some contact with the police during the year of the study, versus 21 and 19 percent for blacks and Hispanics, respectively. Whites were slightly more likely to be involved in police-initiated contact—that is being stopped or approached by police for some reason rather than calling the police yourself—at 12 percent of the white population compared to 11 percent for blacks. Whites also were significantly more likely to initiate contact with police over other racial groups.

One point three million people, or 2 percent of people who had contact with the police in 2018, experienced nonfatal threats or use of force by the police. Broken down by race, that amounted to 2 percent of whites, 4 percent of blacks, and 3 percent of Hispanics who were in contact with police that year. The most common use of force was being handcuffed. Less than 1 percent of members of any race who experienced police contact had a gun pointed at them during their police-initiated contact, according to the Justice Department.

In total since 2015, 6,268 people have been killed by police. 402 of those, or 6 percent, were unarmed. Three percent of people killed by police were unarmed and white and 2 percent were unarmed and black. Out of 61.5 million encounters, that's about twenty unarmed black people a year who are killed by police, a statistic that does not account for situations where police believed they or another individual was in imminent danger or the suspect appeared to be reaching for a weapon but in fact did not have one. The twenty unarmed black men killed by police each year is almost equal to the number of police officers killed in the line of duty by felonious means, between fifteen and twenty officers on average, per year.

Still, any disparity in police-involved killings is explained by crime statistics, which do not exist in the critical race theorist's universe. Whites and Asians commit violent crimes at a much lower rate than their representation in the population. According to 2016 FBI statistics, 59 percent of violent crime arrests were white and 37.5 percent were black. Whites are 76.9 percent of the U.S. population while blacks are 13.3 percent. Blacks commit violent crimes at a rate almost triple what their population percentage would predict.

A study of fatal police shootings that have occurred since 2015 published in the *Proceedings of the National*

Academy of Sciences concluded, "We find no evidence of antiblack or anti-Hispanic disparities across shootings, and white officers are not more likely to shoot minority civilians than nonwhite officers. Instead, race-specific crime strongly predicts civilian race. This suggests that increasing diversity among officers by itself is unlikely to reduce racial disparity in police shootings."

The authors went on to say, "As the proportion of black or Hispanic officers in a FOIS [Fatal Officer Involved Shooting] increases, a person shot is more likely to be black or Hispanic than white, a disparity explained by county demographics; race-specific, county-level violent crime strongly predicts the race of the civilian shot."

Workers, including police officers, are not told that most black people disagree with critical race theory's stance on policing. In his video, Peterson points to a Gallup poll conducted in the summer of 2020 that surveyed more than 36,000 Americans and found 61 percent of blacks would like police to spend about the same amount of time in their communities. A further 20 percent reported they'd want more police in their neighborhoods. That's 81 percent of blacks in favor of policing as it is conducted now.

People remain intensely uncomfortable with this subject. In writing this book I relied on a dozen whistleblowers who spoke to me on condition of anonymity. They came from all walks of life and represented a diverse cross-section of the economy. These were everyday people forced to undergo diversity, equity, and inclusion training on the job and they weren't prepared to speak publicly.

Fear is our most earnest emotion: fear of getting fired, being canceled, losing status, or being perceived as the worst thing in society—a bigot, a racist, a homophobe. This apprehension is the bloodline of Big Diversity's metastasis. Whistleblowers who contacted me increasingly witnessed their mandatory training sessions take a turn toward something destructive and evil that simply didn't belong on the job. They felt they had no one to talk to and nowhere to express their concerns.

Cops are among the most weary. They not only risk deferment but losing their pensions for speaking to a journalist without approval. Frank S., a detective in the New York Police Department, laughed when I asked him about racism in the nation's largest police force. Frank has worked in all five boroughs in his seventeen years with the NYPD. He asked me to use a pseudonym due to rules against officers speaking to journalists without permission and over fear of repercussions from NYPD leadership.

For the NYPD, Frank says, things started to change after the 2014 death of Eric Garner. That's when bureaucrats wearing race goggles who answer to City Hall started making the job more difficult for the rank and file.

Garner, a six-foot-three, three-hundred-fifty-pound Staten Island man, died of a heart attack after resisting arrest for illegally selling loose cigarettes outside a convenience store. The cardiac event was triggered after a police officer placed Garner in a restraint. The slogan "I can't breathe," which he reportedly said eleven times during the altercation with police, originates with Garner. The phrase is now a staple of cable news ledes when the subject is "excessive force." It adorns T-shirts and, unironically, face masks. But law enforcement across the country are also routinely trained that, if a suspect can say the words, "I can't breathe," they, in fact, are breathing—an experiment you can try at home yourself.

Never mind that. "Lose some weight" might have been a better message: Garner probably would still be alive today if he had been a fitter man. A grand jury decided not to indict the officer involved in Garner's death and the city settled with a multi-million-dollar payout to Garner's family.

"99.9 percent of cops all agreed that we would have done the same thing," Frank says of that officer's actions. "How else can you take this huge guy like that down? Even black cops agreed. But, obviously, the guy's in terrible shape. So right away, we went through retraining for that, they wanted to teach us to keep away from using that type of hold. It's not an illegal chokehold, but it's virtually impossible to bring somebody down that's bigger than you unless you have a martial arts expert. So now, any kind of pressure applied to the diaphragm or torso was illegal. They tried the martial arts training, you know, leg takedowns and this type stuff, but that takes years and years to learn. It just wasn't working. So, the approach afterward is just, well, unless somebody's shooting somebody else, or trying to stab them right in front of you, take a hands-off approach to everything."

Diversity training had been around for a while but at that time the department hadn't resorted to telling all police officers that they were racists. Frank recalls taking the same LGBT sensitivity course I attended in 2015. "That was one of the really cool trainings, I'll be honest with you. I remember they asked for volunteers, and they had to step into situations like a domestic situation. So, they want you to approach things from different angles. There are different kinds of relationships out there, and I remember even volunteering. We had a blast, that was a really awesome, fun day," Frank says. "But this other stuff that they're doing now? Oh my God. Wow."

In late 2020 Frank was hauled in with other senior cops for a skin color lecture mandated by the department after the Floyd riots. The course had nothing to do with the basic reality of their jobs, and officers reacted with annoyance and ambivalence. As Frank recalls, it was—simply put—complete bullshit that no one was buying. Unlike other jobs, cops didn't have to pretend to care—they've got a union behind them. It was understood this new training was purely political.

"They go around and ask, 'has anybody in this room experienced racism, raise your hand.' And then they ask, 'if anybody has been racist to somebody, raise your hand.' Of course, no one raises their hand. People are looking at their phones. Then the supervisor says, 'Something I want you all to know, regardless of your skin color on this job, as a police officer you have, since the day you started working.'"

"All the cops start hemming and hawing, and the supervisor goes, 'I'm going to explain to you why every single encounter you've had with people out there is inherently racist.' It just got more and more ridiculous from there. I even remember the only cop who spoke up against it was an Asian guy," Frank says.

The instructor passed out note cards and asked the cops to write down something racist. "And no one did that, either. What's someone going to do, write down the word 'nigger' and be the only one who does it? Now they found their racist, if they were looking for one."

Frank tried to recall if he'd ever witnessed any overt racism in his nearly two decades on the police force. The only incidents he could come up with involved black cops who seemed to have a beef with white people. There was one officer, a former Marine, who grew his beard out at work. Facial hair is prohibited save for religious or medical reasons, and even then, an officer needs a note from a rabbi, imam, or doctor. When his supervisor, who was white, told the black cop to shave it off, he threw a hissy fit. He protested that it was emasculating for a black man to take that kind of order from a white man, despite it being department policy. Eventually a black female captain was called in to tell him to shave his beard. That's not emasculating, apparently, and the officer complied.

Even New York's reviled former mayor, Bill de Blasio, and police commissioner, Dermot Shea, seemed to understand that convincing NYPD officers there was a racism problem in the force wasn't going to go very far. What sort of masochistic white supremacist would choose the unending nightmare of living in New York City—where a tsunami of multiculturalism shoves you down the sidewalk each morning—let alone joining its police force? Sure, there are plenty of combative, rage-addicted people in New York but that might be taking it a bit far.

"No one takes this job because they want to go out there and crack skulls," Frank laughs. "I've never been on an anti-crime team out there and harassing minority kids on the street corner, shaking them down and pulling guns off them, just because they were black. Nobody has ever worked with another cop who's, like, 'yeah, see those black kids over there, let's go search them just because they're black.' It's just nonsense. Everybody would just be looking at you like, 'what are you talking about?'"

Training instead focused on dealing with the public. De-escalation has always been a part of policing, now officers were being told they had to give certain groups a pass. "It's called Excited Delirium Syndrome, it's like 'wilding out,' if you're familiar with that term," Frank says. "It's how certain people react to authority. They were now telling us it's OK for one group to act like that but not another. This is how certain people respond to excitement and you have to be sensitive to that, to the culture. It's not that some people are just individuals and behave like that, it's the culture you have to take into account. You have to be aware of these sorts of things with these different groups of people when you're interacting with them."

"One thing they really emphasized was this statistic that 70 percent of black men will report a negative interaction with the police, or a negative interaction in the past. But they won't talk about homicide rates and who's responsible."

Frank says while cherry-picked statistics that feed into critical race theory were shoved down officer's throats, no statistics about crime rates and race were ever mentioned in any police training he was ever required to take. In fact, they're forbidden.

"Take this anti-Asian hate crime stuff, it's all black men attacking Asians," he says. In the last few months Frank worked nearly every anti-Asian hate crime under investigation by the NYPD. In the final weeks of Trump's presidency, to hit the man they hated so dearly on the way out, mainstream media touted a statistic that anti-Asian attacks in the U.S. were up 150 percent. The reason, the media claimed, was President Trump's aggressive stance on China during the COVID-19 pandemic, which he routinely called the "China virus." I found myself roped into this when Media Matters for America, a leftwing watchdog group, ran a story smearing various commentators as we made light of journalists' hypersensitivity to the term "China virus," suggesting we were responsible for the alleged rise on attacks against Asians.

"Stop calling it COVID-19," I wrote in a tweet picked up by Media Matters. "It's Wu Flu, Kung Flu, Wuhan virus, Bat Soup Bug, Sweet n Sour Sicken, or China virus." It upset all the right people, though I could have gone on to include the Shanghai Shivers, Fu Manchu Fever, Rice Rabies, Lo Mein Pain, Wu-Ping Cough, Mandarin Malady, Wet Market Surprise, Winnie the Flu, and Communist Lung Herpes. Still, imagine my surprise to learn, like the president, I apparently held a lot of sway over violent inner-city blacks, known as they are to go to bat for white, gay conservatives on Twitter who have names like *Chadwick*.

Liberal media salivated at the rise of attacks against Asians in New York, but it turned out to be disastrous for the narrative linking street violence to an increase in white extremism. Out of 18.5 million Asians in the U.S., the 150 percent increase amounted to 122 incidents in 2020 compared to forty-nine in 2019. But hate crime statistics are notoriously unreliable, often dependent on subjective reporting by law enforcement. Crime overall was on the rise in major U.S. cities. The year 2020 was the bloodiest year in New York in nearly a decade. Murders were up 41 percent compared to 2019. Murders were up an additional 36 percent in the first three months of 2021. And the perpetrators were never the race news organizations wanted them to be.

"It's always black. Occasionally, maybe once, it's a white guy who's homeless and threw a bottle at a guy who happened to be Asian, but then we have to mark it down as a hate crime," Frank says.

Since George Floyd, NYPD officers are forbidden from mentioning the race of perpetrators and suspects, even over internal airways. If officers on the street are looking for a suspect who violently assaulted, murdered, or raped someone, "it goes like this: male, six foot one, green jacket, orange sneakers. When you give a description, you can't say what race they are," Frank says. But if it's an attack on an Asian, everyone instinctively knows it's a black guy, he says.

"They purposefully avoid that and crime statistics. Those are hot topics. Instead, they approach everything from this social justice warrior perspective. You know, saying things like, 'So-and-so was arrested for smoking marijuana when he was thirteen or dealing drugs when he was sixteen. He never had a chance. And the neighborhood, it didn't allow him to go to college, and he couldn't go get a government job. That's why he's living off the government now and the only thing he can do is sell drugs.'"

"They'll do everything they can to avoid talking about the real issues. Who is responsible for the majority of robberies in the city? Who's responsible for any one of these violent crimes? They don't allow us to talk about that."

The colorblindness rule doesn't apply to victims. It also seemed to overlook DCPI, the Office of the Deputy Commissioner for Public Information, according to Frank. DCPI deals with the media. It's the police department's public relations operation. Like all PR outfits, DCPI has a you-scratch-my-back-I'll-scratch-yours relationship with news organizations. Each morning someone from DCPI rang up Frank to ask what cases he was working on. In early 2021, DCPI was aware the news outlets wanted anti-Asian assaults and they wanted to pin it on white men, but that didn't exist.

"If I had an assault case against an Asian, they'd ask what the perpetrator looked like. I couldn't say his race, so sometimes they would just flat out ask if he was white. If he's white, they really want to know so they can get that out in the media. That's where the liberal media has their hands in our pockets, because it comes from above. These are the stories certain media outlets want and if they have it, DCPI will call CNN."

I asked Frank how the police department benefitted from that. Why abet the media, who were the biggest perpetrators of cop hatred? "If they give CNN what they want, then we'll get a positive story about us out in return. Something like a cop delivers a baby in the back of a cab, a feel-good story, never crime related, like a rescue job, or a cop raises money for an Iraq vet, or a story about the newest minority being promoted as a chief," he says.

Police weren't just being told that a tendency to "wild out" in front of authority was genetically linked to skin color. The department's antiterrorism training also shifted radically to accommodate the media and progressive fictions du jour. Three years before Floyd's death, Frank attended special antiterrorism training in New

Mexico hosted by the FBI. "The feds that taught that class were spot on," Frank says. "They said to us, 'the media is going to tell you that white people are responsible for the majority of terrorism in this country, but that's false. It's exactly who you think, it's mainly Muslim terrorism.'"

Since September 11, 2001, nine confirmed Islamic terrorist attacks have hit New York City. Five of the nine were thwarted by law enforcement before any lives were lost. The most recent occurred in October 2017 when an Islamic terrorist drove a rented pickup truck down a bike path that runs parallel to the West Side Highway and killed eight people. But three years later, Islamic extremism had been wiped completely from the NYPD's antiterrorism syllabus. Seemingly overnight, all antiterrorism training shifted to white nationalist extremism, a phenomenon in New York City about as prevalent as a black person at a Pete Buttigieg rally.

"The NYPD's angle on everything is geared toward white nationalism now. It's funny when they mention white terrorism they never mention Antifa, though. They call them 'activists' and 'protestors.' But the NYPD has labeled the Proud Boys as domestic terrorists," Frank told me, referring to the multi-ethnic, working class, pro-Trump men's drinking club started by *Vice* magazine founder Gavin McInnes—a group of men I once got to know well and can verify at the time they were anything but white nationalists.

I wondered, in his seventeen years on the force, if Frank ever encountered a white nationalist in New York City. "If there was one, he'd stick out like a sore thumb here. That's just unheard of," he said.

I had to agree. Living in New York for just as long, I suspected someone walking down the street with a swastika tattoo wasn't going to get very far. "But they have us out looking for a Unabomber type. A lone wolf scenario, stuff like that. Some Nazi walking around out there who is a ticking time bomb just waiting to do something. But he's a mythical creature. He's not out there," Frank says.

"The imaginary monster is a distraction from the real problem. He's an excuse to make us look the other way when it comes to work we should be doing: broken windows policing, quality of life, and that kind of crime."

"The quality-of-life stuff, it's funny, because they're kind of apologetic to us about it," Frank says of his supervisors. "They just let us know, this is the way politics is going. This is the future, and the old way of policing is out the window. This is the job now."

Chapter Two
Meet Your Diversity Czar:
A Rogues' Gallery of DEI Consultants

D iversity, Equity and Inclusion might be the first Marxist cultural revolution that's also a business. Your workplace may have its own in-house diversity czar or your job may outsource the business to a firm specializing in intraoffice skin tone relations.

For those firms, a leap into diversity and inclusion is framed as an investment but not one with any actual returns. *Companies that invest in DEI see increased productivity and employee satisfaction,* goes the pitch. "The most ethnically diverse companies are 35% more likely to perform better than the least ethnically diverse companies," one DEI firm, called Holistic Inclusion Consulting, claims on its website. There's no source listed for that statistic nor any clear definition of what, exactly, "more likely to perform better" means. DEI consultants routinely appropriate business lingo they don't understand—words like "investment," "performance," or "portfolio"—when selling their services to corporations. And they don't need to: No business seeks out a DEI regimen because they believe it increases productivity. It's a political safeguard.

Another DEI firm, called Equity at the Center, prepares organizations to expect an initial investment followed by an annual subscription. Once you take the plunge to become a better corporate citizen, it's a lifelong commitment. "Building a Race Equity Culture is an ongoing process that requires a significant investment in time and financial resources," the group says on its website, "most organizations invested primarily in consultants to help them articulate their goals and priorities for this work and to support them through coaching and mentoring."

A sample "investment" listed on the group's website highlights a client called Organization B, which can claim five years of active commitment to "the work." Organization B's initial annual investment in "race equity capacity building" clocked in at $700,000. Its current annual investment is "unavailable." Since "the work"—which sounds like something that happened in Jonestown—began, Organization B's staff swelled from ten people to 150 people. It's unclear what this staff up means, but Equity at the Center felt it was important to highlight, nonetheless. Another client, Organization A, is identified as paying an activation fee to Equity at the Center between $20,000 to $40,000 with an annual subscription rate of $10,000 to $20,000. Eight years on from plugging into the DEI grift, Organization A's staff increased from 200 to 750, according to the report.

For free-range race hustlers brought in to indoctrinate your staff on the tenets of a Maoist revolution, a range of fees may apply. For the busy revolutionary, Netta Jenkins of Holistic Inclusion Consulting offers an online go-at-your-own-pace course for 50 percent off the retail asking price of $399. Jenkins' discount sessions include discussions on "antiracism, product inclusion, and systemic bias globally."

Jenkins is an industry star, but the industry also offers lesser-knowns like Torin Perez, who states he's on a "mission to inspire authenticity and inclusive leadership in the workplace" and offers a price list for his services, ranging from $10,000 to $100,000. "Fees may vary based on options selected above," the site reads, where customers can choose from consulting, speaking, and training work. Like most diversity consultants, Perez's qualifications seem to be little more than, *I'm black and people have paid me to do this before.* That, and he once worked in advertising for Bloomberg LP.

Whether you meet your diversity czar in a teleconference, a board room, or a lavish corporate retreat, you can make a few assumptions about the person charged to speak about diversity and inclusion to your company. Just don't assume their gender. For answers to that, check any electronic communication you've received from this person—it has a 100 percent chance of listing pronouns in the signature. You'll also find their pronouns on all social media, in text messages, maybe they'll even tattoo them somewhere on their body or billboard them across an article of clothing, like on their face mask. Pronoun diligence, boarding on psychopathy, is a hallmark of the diversity czar's pettiness and defalcation. Actually, they don't deserve the "psychopathy" description, as that implies danger and mystique. Psychopaths are interesting; these people are not.

One can still draw up a taxonomy though as diversity czars fit into five categories of detestable reject you'll encounter in the workplace: the Masochists, the Parasites, the Saviors, the Born Losers, and the Randos.

The Rando

A boutique industry has sprouted up offering race training certifications, but no actual qualifications are required to grieve and complain to a room full of strangers. It was the case with Sam, who works for a national bank in St. Louis, Missouri, that just any random black person would do. Sam is a team leader in the IT department. He asked me to use a pseudonym and to withhold the name of his company over concerns that speaking about his job's DEI policies may get him fired.

While America's cities were rocked by race riots following the death of George Floyd, Sam's company sent out an email to team leaders. The suits wanted racial unrest to be discussed on company time but they needed someone black to do it. Sam, who is white, was among employees tasked with identifying black coworkers and asking those employees if they'd be willing to give a lecture on race to the office.

Sam was horrified and he refused. "I said, if I need to be written up for that, I'm perfectly fine with that because I will take it to the ACLU. It was the most insulting thing I have ever heard and I couldn't believe that this company is speaking like this in this day and age," he told me.

Employees were still working remotely due to COVID-19 restrictions. It was a large company; many had never met. As one team leader put it sotto voce to Sam, "Like, seriously, how do we identify who is black?"

Corporate came up with an answer: Go through their team directory and retrieve human resources reports and look at employee photos to determine their race. "So, she did that, and then she reached out to these employees and said, 'Next time we have a meeting can you talk about George Floyd or something?'"

"And, exactly as I had responded, they were offended. They were like, 'Why are you asking me to talk about this?'"

Three weeks passed and Sam had mostly forgotten about the directive. One day during a teleconference a black woman appeared on screen to berate the staff, ranting about George Floyd and policing in black communities. "This is enough! This has got to stop!" the woman shouted to a shaken and bewildered IT department.

For all Sam knew, the angry woman could have been a teller in Cleveland, a janitor in Wichita, or just someone off the street. "No one knew who this woman was, they just found someone," Sam said. "This wasn't just our continental U.S. team. We had people from India and the Philippines on that meeting. I couldn't believe we were sitting here being forced to listen to this bullshit. They were shoving the stupid narrative down our throats."

The Born Loser

Likely to be your company's full time Diversity and Inclusion Officer, the Born Loser is the most pathetic but least threatening of the czars. He likely was once a true believer in the mission of the race monger industry. Words like "justice" and "equality" stirred a sense of purpose in the Born Loser, who always felt adrift and invisible. Somewhere along the way, the Born Loser stumbled upon an explanation for all his misgivings, ineptitudes, and the way everyone seemed to recoil from him. It must be due to something immutable like his race or sexuality. Wherever he went, he craved acceptance and celebration but only on his terms. Lacking self-awareness and grit, but plump with self-pity, he never wanted anything badly enough if it meant he, not others, was the problem.

The American education system envelops people like this in a warm, gardenia-scented grandmother's hug of unconditional love and support. They're primed to be educators and other in-the-trenches revolutionaries. His academic pursuits taught him deeper, wackier definitions of "justice" and "equality," and lots of other words, too. His sense of history got warped. His interpretation of the humanities became less human and more chilling, mechanical, and hierarchical. Where others might find beauty, wonder, or nuance, he saw entitlement. How could such things be valued while *injustice* lurked somewhere, anywhere.

The Born Loser's feelings of inadequacy metastasized into a fastidious, monomaniacal pursuit of what makes people different, rather than the same, of material good versus material evil, of oppressor and oppressed. This inevitably led the Born Loser into leftist philosophizing—that mankind and their systems can be engineered to perfection, that utopia is in our grasp with the right planning. Perfection, however, is subjective to the experiences and desires of the Born Loser, who really isn't all that sure himself of what a paradisiac, just world looks like. He just knows this isn't it. Everything comes down to questions of fairness, of what people are owed. As a child, he got his way by being annoying and pitied, and he carried that into adulthood. He ended up the worst kind of tyrant, the one whose name you can't remember. He didn't stoke fear but exasperation. Rather than love and human connection—where most people find happiness—his self-worth got tied to frivolous, impotent victories of minute intimidation.

He was probably an average pupil, even in classes where he ought to have excelled—Women's Studies, African American Studies, Indigenous Queer Studies, Laplander Interpretive Dance Studies, Feminist Ice Fishing, Racism and the Papua New Guinea Diaspora Studies, etc. He remained lazy, casually obsessed with his own ineptitude, and spent most nights snacking in front of the television while his roommates were out having fun and getting laid. Still, he was determined to be a catalyst for change in the world, just not a very big one, because that might take a lot of work and just a little bravado.

Middle management might be a calling, and perhaps he tried that, but the job didn't offer enough opportunities to make other people feel bad. He somehow wound his way into the role of Diversity and Inclusion Officer at Company X. The fat salary and lifetime job security soon weren't enough to turn our restless Born Loser gracious. After a few years on the job, dark suspicions settled in. Perhaps this was all guff. Perhaps he really didn't have much to offer.

That's how you're likely to find your Born Loser diversity czar—passionless, no longer the protagonist of even his own story but reduced to the corporate equivalent of a sidewalk permit. Resignation becomes a lifestyle, not just a circumstance. He eventually will strive for joy in his personal life, perhaps in collecting things—like doll parts or old perfume bottles—and, of course, each day holds the promise of some other, unexpected thrill, like berating the dry cleaner or shaming a waiter into a free dessert.

The Savior

In the totem pole of viciousness, the Savior's gruesome Hannya grin takes the middle slot. Usually—probably always—a white woman or male homosexual, a few assumptions can be made about this breed of czar. You can bet she refers to her husband as her "partner" and he's almost guaranteed to be Of Color, just not black. Even if she weren't privately terrified of black men, which she is, she wouldn't have been able to find one who'd put up with her domineering and condescending ways. He's probably Asian, Indian, vaguely Middle Eastern, or a castrated Hispanic and, like most people, doesn't like her too much but found a cushy nook to inhabit in her maniacal, zealous empire of caregiving.

The Savior isn't very political—politics are too grimy—but she does know that No Human Is Illegal, Love Is Love, and Science Is Real. She never came upon a hand-carved Live, Laugh, Love wall decoration she didn't appreciate. Whirlwind shopping trips to T.J. Maxx and treasure hunting at Goodwill stave off her tendency toward substance abuse. That, and nurturing the world. She is needed, and for that reason she must always be *on*.

She studied social work, psychology, or child development and may work in those fields when not explaining to your accounting department what a microaggression is. She subscribes to lots of journals and prides herself on keeping up to date on the latest studies and lingo. She's here to take on your problems, but only after hers have been tucked away and sealed for the day. All she really wants from life is for people to be vulnerable and cry in front of her, but she saves her own crying for a twisted, heaving, full-blown meltdown once a month alone in the shower—a ghastly ruckus her partner and the kids have learned to just ignore. There's no such thing as a dumb question and wherever she goes—in the office, in the checkout lane, sitting in traffic—her self-assured aura of tender strength says *I am present and I care.*

The Parasite

What image comes to mind when you see the word *parasite*? A plump little bloodsucker clinging to your dog's ass? A microbe inhabiting a galaxy of shit gorging on nutrients supplied by an unwitting host? While both descriptions are helpful when thinking of diversity czars, parasites in nature take many forms. Parasites are often cunning hustlers, vengeful brutes, and Mafiosi. They may be experts at exploiting loopholes and vulnerabilities or taking advantage of the good nature and hard work of others. This is their survival strategy, and it works as long as they're allowed to continue the scam. It is, in a sense, a more respectable existence than we find in the Born Loser or the Savior. The Diversity Parasite has moxie, and you fell for it.

The parasitic diversity czar is a more dastardly type of freeloader than any organism lurking in a churro you bought from a tiny Hispanic woman on the subway. Consider, instead, the North American brown-headed cowbird. The brown-headed cowbird, or *Molothrus ater*, is a member of the blackbird family and one of several bird species known as brood parasites. With more than 220 known targeted host species, the brown-headed cowbird is one of the most prolific parasites in the world.

Birds are famously loving and attentive parents. Many species mate for life. Females may spend weeks sitting on the nest without budging; males work tirelessly providing food and protection for the entire family. Bird families are tight, cohesive, and industrious. The brown-headed cowbird, on the other hand, is not. She doesn't build, she destroys. She looks around covetously at her bird neighbors—happy, productive, betrothed robins, hummingbirds, yellow warblers, brown thrashers, and gray catbirds—and says, *I'm going to burn that shit to the ground.*

The brown-headed cowbird learns the comings and goings of her expectant bird neighbors. When the nest of another species is left unattended, she swoops in and plops a few of her own eggs into the brood. Her eggs hatch sooner, and her chicks grow faster than those of the host species. They gobble up all the energy and resources of the host parents. When it's all over, after the cowbird chicks have starved their nestmates to death and exhausted the parents, they flap off to lay waste to the next happy, unsuspecting nest. If a host species spots the deception and destroys the interloping brown-headed cowbird's eggs, the brown-headed cowbird mother will retaliate by destroying the host birds' own eggs and smashing up the nest.

That's the avian equivalent of crying racism in the workplace if someone refuses to take on your scam. The parasitic diversity czar knows the game and plays it masterfully. They know their targets better than those targets know themselves, and they always get what they want in the end.

These are your critical race glitterati—the Nikole Hannah-Joneses and Ibram X. Kendis who stalk the halls of universities, newspapers, and the Big Tech and Pharma companies. They're plenty available for corporate retreats and race seminars. The free-market rewards them with fame and fortune for the service of trashing the free market. They thrive on white guilt and white masochism.

"The life of racism cannot be separated from the life of capitalism," Kendi writes in one of his books. "In order to truly be antiracist, you also have to truly be anticapitalist." Kendi might be the biggest antiantiracist of all then. He charges $20,000 an hour for virtual presentations. According to the *New York Post*, he's "merchandised his entire line of ideas, releasing self-help products and even an 'antiracist' baby book. He gratefully accepts millions from tech and pharmaceutical companies on behalf of his Antiracism Center." "Fighting Big Capital," the *Post* writer commented, "is a lucrative enterprise."

Perhaps Kendi fights racism by sucking cash from institutionalized white supremacy and putting it directly in the pockets of one black man. "There is no such thing as a nonracist or race-neutral policy. If discrimination is creating equity, then it is antiracist. If discrimination is creating inequity, then it is racist," Kendi writes in his most popular book, *How to Be an Antiracist*.

Kendi, you see, has always been a victim of racism. Son of a mother working as a business analyst for a healthcare organization and a tax accountant father, he grew up middle-class. He attended private schools in New York City before moving to Virginia where he went to a top high school. Racism followed him throughout his careers at the State University of New York-Oneonta, SUNY Albany, Brown University, the University of Florida, Florida A&M University, Temple University, American University in Washington, D.C., Harvard University, and Boston University, where he currently teaches.

But racism wasn't done with Kendi. Like a parrot on his shoulder constantly squawking the n-word, racism followed him relentlessly on national television appearances, at prestigious fellowships, and as he signed lucrative book deals with gilded publishing houses such as Macmillan, Nation Books, and Little, Brown. Then racism lay in waiting as his books landed at the top of the *New York Times* bestseller list.

While the Parasite commits the most carnage, he hardly can be faulted. He might be vicious and immoral, but like the brown-headed cowbird, why give up such a profitable grift if no one has the fortitude to stop you?

The Masochist

I was weeks into my journey through diversity and inclusion training before I realized one of the industry's most festooned templars, Robin DiAngelo, author of *White Fragility,* is white! *Finally, some diversity*, I thought. DiAngelo is not a Savior, the role you expect white women to take on in the DEI corporate-industrial complex. She's a gnarled entity plagued by delusions of mighty evil lurking deep within herself that must be extracted and whipped, analyzed then torched, contained, monitored, feared and studied, discussed, considered, forever. This evil known as white supremacy cannot be conventionally slayed. Like the ghost of Voldemort it is shapeless and ethereal, a black mist choking the soul.

One hand guides the other hand to slap one's own face for all of time—this is the Masochist's song. Another word for that is narcissism. "I grew up poor and white. While my class oppression has been relatively visible to me, my race privilege has not. In my efforts to uncover how race has shaped my life, I have gained deeper insight by placing race in the center of my analysis and asking how each of my other group locations have socialized me to collude with racism," DiAngelo has said of her upbringing.

"In so doing, I have been able to address in greater depth my multiple locations and how they function together to hold racism in place. I now make the distinction that I grew up poor and white, for my experience of poverty would have been different had I not been white."

DiAngelo has a PhD in Multicultural Education, and her areas of expertise are Whiteness Studies, which we assume isn't about European Art during the Renaissance, and Critical Discourse Analysis—whatever the fuck that is. In an academic article in 2011 she coined the term "white fragility," which she went on to flesh out in a well-timed *New York Times* bestseller seven years later. On her website, under a page called "Accountability," DiAngelo discusses continual education for white people on their privilege and antiracist behaviors, setting herself up, like most DEI hawks, for continued relevance and steady income.

But as a Masochist, she must first discount herself at length. "But the foundation of our education must be rooted in the voices and perspectives of Black, Indigenous, and Peoples of Color. We will never understand racism in isolation....

"Accountability within antiracist work is the understanding that what I profess to value must be demonstrated in action, and the validity of that action is determined by Black, Indigenous, and Peoples of Color. Accountability requires trust, transparency, and action. As a white person seeking to be accountable, I must continually ask myself, 'How do I know how I am doing?' To answer this question, I need to check in and find out. I can do this in several ways, including: by directly asking Black, Indigenous, and Peoples of Color with whom I have trusting relationships and who have agreed to offer me this feedback."

All white liberals are ethno-masochists. They'll read someone like Kendi because they feel like they *should*, but they don't enjoy it. He may have dark skin, but Kendi isn't really black. He's culturally white. He speaks the language of the white liberal but without any of the guilt. He's someone white liberals revere, and that's about it. They can't relate to him, but neither can most black people, for that matter. But throw them the juicy bad conscience of a middle-aged white woman and they're as weak-kneed as Stacey Abrams at a Golden Corral.

Unlike the Savior, the Masochist does not carry your burdens, but her own, and for that you need to pay her. Professional self-flagellation doesn't come cheap, but the flogger will ensure it's as hassle-free as possible—at least for her. For $15,000 DiAngelo won't even put on pants. According to the *Washington Free Beacon* that's what she charges for virtual speaking engagements. DiAngelo recently lowered the cost to $12,500 for a public university. How very generous. But when the university asked her to consider $10,000, she declined. The *Free Beacon* reported the school eventually agreed to the $12,500 price tag and DiAngelo still couldn't be bothered to give a live demonstration. She cashed the check and sent a prerecorded speech.

Like alcoholism, DiAngelo's skin color is an innate spiritual malady that manifests in destructive, real-world behaviors. Because your whiteness can only be kept in check and never cured, DiAngelo offers a twelve-step program on her website to keep yourself accountable.

Step One reminds you to always write those checks: "Donate a percentage of your income to racial justice organizations led by BIPOC people. If you earn more than enough to meet your basic economic needs, strive to give until you can 'feel it.' Your checkbook is a reflection of your antiracist commitment made tangible through directly addressing the unjust distribution of economic resources based on race."

Step Eight: "Attend white affinity groups. In an affinity group, people who share the same racial identity meet on a regular basis to address the challenges specific to their group," it instructs.

(Just be careful not to get too carried away in your white affinity group, because we once called that the Klan).

Step Nine reminds you this journey will follow you to the grave. "Never consider your learning finished. Continually participate in every racial justice education forum you can (conference, workshops, talks). Continually read and learn from the work of BIPOC people. Take online classes taught by BIPOC people," she writes, using the redundant acronym "BIPOC people" twice, like writing "ATM machine" or "HIV virus," further displaying her profound feeble-mindedness, in case you weren't already convinced.

Chapter Three
A New, Stupid Way of Thinking: Mastering the Lingo of Your Sunny Overlords

An article published in *Diversity Officer Magazine* traces the origins of diversity training in the United States to the 1960s. Diversity education—particularly in the U.S. military sectors, where it became ubiquitous—arrived in reaction to the civil rights movement. It soon spread to other organizations, communities, and to higher education. Social upheaval at the time became the rationale for the programs intended to increase racial sensitivity between black and white Americans, with the goal of organizational cohesion.

"The military employed encounter groups in what is perhaps the largest scale diversity education experiment ever conducted. Many of the facilitators viewed the 'encounter' among racial group[s] participating in diversity training as successful when at least one white American admitted that he or she was racist and tearful about racial discrimination and white supremacy," the article describes.

"Employing a black-white pair of facilitators was considered essential for exposing participants to the two-r? relations perspective and to model cross-racial collabor

The facilitators were typically men, and the white facilitator was most valued if he could openly show emotions about his own journey in discovering his deep-seated racism.... Confronting white Americans who made excuses for, or denied their racism, was common in this diversity training approach. The goal was to increase white American sensitivity to the effects of racial inequity."

Participants soon reported very negative reactions to this type of training—with some indicators suggesting it made people more racist. The Defense Department's Race Relations Institute soon dropped the 'encounter' groups and curtailed hours spent on diversity education. According to the magazine, in the 1970s and 1980s, with the women's liberation movement and the sexual revolution, gender education became part of the curriculum in diversity efforts across the private and public sectors. In the 1990s, gays and lesbians entered the syllabus. In the new millennium, transgenders and gender identity came into the fold.

In 2020, after Democrats seized both Congress and the White House, Diversity and Inclusion offices at companies across the country quietly changed their names to The Office of Diversity, Equity, and Inclusion. Even before taking office the Biden administration promised to make equity its top priority. The word equality signifies fairness in opportunity. Equity means revenge. Your company may have assessed a legal risk/benefit analysis in enforcing diversity protocols; feared retaliation from touchy millennials; has stupid people in charge who read too much *New York Times*; or implemented diversity training just because it sounded like a harmless thing to do, like a company picnic or letting someone's kids sell Girl Scout Cookies at the office—sorry, Nonbinary Child Scout Cookies. But the shift to equity is about cozying up to power.

The concept of equity is divorced from racial equality, but in a way the forces of diversity hope you won't notice.

The old school liberal cried for equality but equality, it turns out, was a bit too conservative in practice, was pretty much already in place and, for the left, was nauseatingly in step with the U.S. Constitution. Powered by grievance and bullying, equity is mean-spirited and destructive. It is the green-eyed, incremental seizure and redistribution of all resources and opportunities based on fluid and ever-changing criteria determined by an elite few at the top who will never feel its consequences. Equality might empower individuals, but equity empowers those in charge. Equity—drilled into workplace consciousness in a deluge of corporate-ese and the chilling Helvetica of a PowerPoint presentation—means socialism. But the word itself sounds so close to equality most people haven't noticed—and if they did, assumed the two were interchangeable.

Diversity, equity, and inclusion training will expose you to a way of seeing the world that might seem counterintuitive to everything you've picked up by simply living in a society filled with lots of different types of people. Instruction may seem bizarre, stupid, racist, or flat-out incorrect and that's the point. DEI teaches a false reality. If you can convince a society that the sky is red—or men are actually women, or that America is a hateful country—you can make them believe anything. This begins with taking control over language. To construct a reality, you must establish a terminology and point of view.

Casey Peterson, the Sandia National Laboratories whistleblower, learned that in 2019, when his workplace hosted an event at a luxury resort for white male executives called the "White Men's Caucus on Illuminating Racism, Sexism, and Homophobia in Organizations." Diversity trainers demanded the men make a list of things they associated with white male culture. They ended up with lists heavy on white supremacists, the Ku Klux Klan, Aryan Nation, MAGA hats, privilege, and mass killings. The trainers insisted white males must work hard to understand their white privilege, male privilege, and heterosexual privilege and expose the roots of white male culture, "which consists of rugged individualism, a can-do attitude, hard work, and striving toward success," traits "which [sound] good, but are in fact devastating to women and people of color," Peterson attested in a video posted to YouTube.

The trainers claimed, "white male culture leads to lower quality of life at work and home" and causes "reduced life expectancy, unproductive relationships, and high stress. It also forces this white male standard on women and minorities. In a subsequent session, the white males must publicly recite the series of white privilege statements and male privilege statements. They must accept their complacency in the white male system and their role in creating oppressions," Peterson said.

"Finally, as re-education camp concludes, the white males must write letters directed to white women, people of color, and other groups regarding the meaning of this caucus experience. They apologized for their privilege and pledged to become better allies."

That retreat was reportedly hosted by a company called White Men as Full Diversity Partners. Materials obtained by Christopher Rufo of the Discovery Institute listed "examples of white male culture," including "golf," "quick decisions," "self-confident [sic]," "risk-taking," and "brave" in the training document. Words are very important in the diversity squad. They'll be used to isolate and humiliate one group at the expense of elevating another. In diversity class you'll be expected to learn the lingo. What follows is a handy guide to some of the key concepts of the DEI mindset.

Accountability

Put down your Mint Julep, Whitey, it's time for a spanking. America is a terribly racist place and it's all your fault. As long as people like you are here, the Land of the Free will never be fair and equitable. Unfortunately, genocide is off the table for the time being. As an alternative, it's the back of the bus for you, where you're required to take stock of how terrible you are. This will involve a strict regimen of spiritual and psychological flogging, which is exactly what you deserve. In DEI training, we call this process Accountability.

Accountability is not only a personal process. It's everyone's responsibility to hold *each other* accountable. The process of Accountability empowers busybodies, buttinskies, hall monitors, and liberal occultists to pursue a reign of terror around the office, all in the name of keeping everyone accountable. This is how Accountability maintains the DEI brainwashing regime over time and allows its adherents to continually seek out new ways to be accountable.

Accountability also acts as your history lesson. During this process, the 400-year-old bones of dead slaves and warfaring Indian tribes will be dredged up and plopped down on your desk to ponder.

"Greetings my name is Kellie Richardson and I use *she* and *her* pronouns," one webinar on DEI Accountability from an organization called TREC begins. "I'm joining you today from the lands of the Puyallup people, which after generations of settlers is known to many people today as Tacoma, Washington."

"Accountability refers to the ways in which individuals and communities hold themselves to their goals and actions and acknowledge the values and groups to which they are responsible. Accountability demands commitment," she says.

Those responsibilities are never explained, because Accountability does not require them to be real. "Its purpose is to hold us to either perceived or real responsibilities to others," Richardson says. The diversity consultant is so drunk on power, and so accustomed to immunity from criticism, that they breathlessly instruct classrooms on holding accountability to a *perceived* responsibility to another person, whether or not that responsibility actually exists or the person asked for it.

"Accountability can be externally imposed—legal or organization requirements—or internally applied—moral, relational, faith-based, or recognized as some combination of the two on a continuum from the institutional and organizational level to the individual level," she explains. "Accountability is a rich opportunity to monitor progress and consistently identify additional opportunities for DEI learning and growth."

Accountability is a sinister gobbledygook disguised as respectfulness and sensitivity. The ideally accountable worker is toxically feminine—the female psyche at its most disjointed—a hellish state drowned by feelings and subjectivity.

Big "B" Black

That's not a typo. The word "black" is now capitalized. George Floyd's death did indeed change the world but not in a way that annoyed neo-Nazis but rather grammar Nazis. On July 5, 2020, citing Floydian unrest, the *New York Times* published an article explaining why, going forward, the most uptight and conservative style guide in the country would be capitalizing the word "black" in reference to skin color.

The last time the *Times* made a sweeping change to how it referred to black people was ninety years ago. In response to a letter-writing campaign by W.E.B. Du Bois, in 1930 the *Times* promised it would start capitalizing the N in Negro. According to the *Times*, both the N in Negro in 1930 and the B in Black in 2020 would be capitalized "when describing people and cultures of African origin." This time the change was not made in response to an organized campaign or any kind of authentic grassroots demand. Like the rest of the diversity and equity movement it was imposed not from the bottom up but from the top down.

"We believe this style best conveys elements of shared history and identity, and reflects our goal to be respectful of all the people and communities we cover," said Dean Baquet, the *Times*'s executive editor, who appears black but is culturally white.

"It seems like such a minor change, black versus Black," the *Times*'s National editor, Marc Lacey, said to staff. "But for many people the capitalization of that one letter is the difference between a color and a culture."

Never mind that absolutely nothing about black American culture is African in origin. Black American culture is rooted in the white, Scots Irish border-lander culture that was dominant in areas of Appalachia and the Deep South. That's why white rednecks and urban blacks have more in common, culturally, than any other two groups in the U.S., from food, to music, to religion, to slang, to turf wars and tribalism, to a disdain and mistrust of authority. But no one at the *Times* would know that—including its black editors and writers. They've never spent serious time around either group. They are all products of the same elite white liberal academic and professional culture.

The *Times* went on to say that it makes sense to capitalize the B in Black because Latino and Asian are also capitalized. It didn't occur to anyone that black is an adjective while Latin and Asia are proper nouns. Asian, like Hispanic or Latino, is capitalized for the same reason African American is and always has been.

But the *Times* wasn't finished there. "The *Times* also looked at whether to capitalize white and brown in reference to race, but both will remain lowercase. Brown has generally been used to describe a wide range of cultures," Baquet wrote in a memo to staff. "As a result, its meaning can be unclear to readers; white doesn't represent a shared culture and history in the way Black does, and also has long been capitalized by hate groups."

That's funny. Try asking a Nigerian or Jamaican immigrant about his shared culture with a single black mother in Compton and you're likely to get an earful of some of the most racist things you've ever heard in your life. You can also ask the Rwandan Hutus about their shared identity with the Tutsis who murdered them wholesale in a horrifying episode of intertribal hatred and see what that dredges up.

After the *Times* decree, overnight, capital "B" Black became standard in nearly all media style guides across the country and indeed the Western world. Capital "W" White soon followed with many outlets opting for capital "B" Brown as well. It not only makes for awkward reading, it's a powerful tool in creating a sense of opposition between groups of capital "A" Americans. A Black man killed by a White police officer is a more tense situation on the page than that same black man being killed by a white police officer. Just don't expect to find a Black man killing or assaulting an Asian woman in those same pages. In that case he's a colorless figure of mystery linked to no shared collective identity.

Being Color Brave

On May 29, 2018, Starbucks shuttered its eight thousand stores in the U.S. for an emergency diversity and inclusion seminar for the company's one hundred and seventy-five thousand employees. The coffee giant had come under fire for an incident involving two black men at a Philadelphia store who were asked to leave when they would not make a purchase. The two men refused and were subsequently arrested. Protests erupted nationwide at Starbucks locations. The day of racial reckoning for Starbucks employees reportedly cost the company $12 million.

Huddled around iPads at stores across the country, workers sat through dozens of videos about race relations in the U.S. None defined how trespassing is defined in the law. Instead, Starbucks CEO Kevin Johnson told employees "Prejudice in public accommodation is deeply rooted in America."

"Growing up, this term called 'color blind' described a learning behavior pretending not to notice race. That doesn't even make sense. So today we're starting a new journey, talking about race directly," the kindly, gray-haired white man in a plum-colored sweater said, "being color brave."

A Mexican woman working at a Starbucks in San Jose, California, later reflected on the funny new term to a *Time* magazine reporter. "They told us we need to be 'color brave' instead of color blind and it was the whitest thing I've ever heard," she said. "Me and my coworkers of color felt uncomfortable the entire time."

Color blindness is an agent of white supremacy. According to *Outkick*, an anonymous whistleblower at Under Armour, the athletic clothing company based in Baltimore, Maryland, reported that white employees were forced to undergo antiracist trainings in the spring of 2020. The employee came forward to talk about the trainings, entitled "Above the Surface: Dominant White Progressive Narratives." During the sessions, the moderator bizarrely insinuated that for a white person to not attend the funeral of a minority is racist. The moderator also told workers the phrase, "I was taught to treat everyone the same" is racist and that parents who want to send their children to "good schools" are a product of racism. Confronted with such objectively bizarre and meaningless statements, the majority of program participants sat dumbfounded, afraid to say anything.

Across the diversity, equity, and inclusion curriculum, those who claim to avoid paying attention to skin color, or advocate for living in a color-blind society, are advancing racism. Dr. Martin Luther King, Jr., may have had a dream, something to do with judging people by their character, not color, but apparently that dream was whispered into his ear one night by a Grand Wizard of the KKK. Any failure to obsess over skin color in all your interactions and meditations means you are complicit in prolonging a system of racial oppression.

What is this system and how did it come about? Your diversity czar isn't likely to be a historian, but she will rely on false interpretations of U.S. history to become an evangelist about the pervasiveness of white supremacy. The best thing they've got, presently, is a deeply unserious and inexplicably influential *New York Times Magazine* issue titled "The 1619 Project." (One entire issue of the magazine was turned over to 1619 content). Published in August 2019 and overseen by critical race parasite Nikole Hannah-Jones, the special issue attempts to retell the story of America's founding as centered around a queer thing that happened in the year 1619 when a group of about two dozen indentured servants from Africa arrived on a boat in the Chesapeake Bay area. Hannah-Jones makes the wild, false claims that the American Revolution was fought to preserve the institution of slavery and that modern police forces originated in antebellum slave-catching patrol, and then goes on to suggest Abraham Lincoln was a white supremacist.

It won a Pulitzer. Hundreds of thousands of copies were reprinted and distributed to schools and libraries. It was turned into a book and a curriculum. The *Times* advertised *The 1619 Project* during the Superbowl. During the 2020 race riots, vandals scrawled "1619" in spray paint on buildings and statues throughout progressive strongholds. All this despite the fact that the work continues to be debunked by dozens of historians. Competing leftwing news organizations say it needs clarifications and corrections, noting that it dispenses with basic facts of American history. Even the Socialist Equality Party blasted the project, decrying the American left's "shift from class to identity."

Intersectionality

Smoke a joint and put on some Pink Floyd because things are about to get weird. Let a black, nonbinary, fat, disabled, transgender, Muslim, immigrant, HIV-positive prostitute with a peanut allergy take you on a journey through multidimensional oppression using an analytical framework of social and political identities that combine into different modes of privilege and discrimination.

Intersectionality is the *Fear and Loathing in Las Vegas* of the diversity syllabus. This is where you step behind the looking glass to see interlocking systems of power and marginalization where no identity exists in isolation but as part of a swirling, cosmic soup of race, gender, caste, religion, ethnicity, disability, and physical appearance.

LGBTQ+

While we all know what the LGBT stands for, no one is quite sure what the Q means. By most accounts, it's either Questioning—someone titillated by the idea of a same-sex liaison but not quite ready to take the plunge, what we used to call a closet case—or it means Queer. Queers can be divided into two categories. The Type 1 Queer is your everyday homosexual who wants to add a little flair to his persuasion. He fancies his queer identity as "punk rock" and a "fuck you" to The Man. The Queer isn't one to fit into your heteronormative stereotypes. He's special and interesting. His pronouns tell you he is not one, but multitudes. He has a liberal arts degree. His Instagram bio says "Brooklyn-based artist/choreographer/ designer/photographer/DJ/creative director/plant dad" but his tax return says barista. He paints his nails black and wears one dangly earring. He might throw on a wrestling onesie one day and a pleated skirt the next, all to challenge your preconceptions. He likes doing that. He's not going to be put into a box. But at the end of the day, he's just another gay guy who sucks cock and loves Dua Lipa.

The Type 2 Queer just means straight, but with pizzazz. It's the culturally appropriating heterosexual virtue-signaler. The straight female Queer is thoroughly basic. She likes Taylor Swift and the TV show *Friends*. Autumn is her time of year—the chill in the air, the pumpkin spice confectionaries, trips to the apple orchard, knit layers, reflection. While there's nothing wrong with being basic, she's convinced there is. She might have experimented with a green streak of dye in her hair or have a tiny tattoo in a racy spot. She probably goes through lots of phases, fashion wise. She might be quite attractive or fat and frumpy, but for whatever reason she wishes she had unconventional impulses but just doesn't. She's always loved the gays—they're nonthreatening, "fabulous," and she doesn't feel competitive with them. They may treat her poorly. No matter how many times they've stood her up on her birthday or been late for drinks because a Grindr hookup took priority, she stands by her bois.

The Q opened a door for her to become one of them, at least in her mind. For the straight Queers, the Q means there's something far back in their psyche that somewhere along the way led them to believe they're different from all those other straight people, or so they want you to think. Perhaps it was a same-sex snog once in college, or a choking fantasy, or just being, like, really down with transgenders.

The Type 2 Queer eventually will be pressed on which part of the alphabet, exactly, she belongs. This is where the plus comes in. LGBTQ+ is commonly expanded to LGBTQAI2S++, or Lesbian, Gay, Bisexual, Transgender, Queer/Questioning, Asexual, Intersex, Two-Spirit, Plus, Plus. Note, when you extrapolate the plus in LGBTQ+, you get more pluses. Our heterosexual Type 2 Queer lives far down the alphabet in that second plus. The term "demisexual" was made for her. A demisexual is someone who professes to only have sexual feelings toward people she feels an emotional connection. It just means normal, healthy straight woman sexuality. She had a great relationship with her father and a childhood free of trauma. But "demisexual" sounds mystical, like something that came from beyond the Narrow Sea and charms dragons.

The Type 2 Queer may also claim to be polyamorous, having multiple romantic partners at the same time. It means slut, or someone deeply afraid of commitment, but she's neither of those. She knows quite well she'll end up marrying someone who works in finance, move to the suburbs, and have at least two children and a happy life. The Type 2 Queer identity eventually fades away into nothing more than a Facebook memory. When that happens, the gay friends stop coming around. Having moved on from the alphabet for a life more grounded and rewarding, she may on occasion try to relive those old days, maybe by starting a Drag Queen Story Hour at her local public library, or imagining she's very close with the local hairdresser, who's never once seen her outside the salon.

Type 2 Queers may also be, although rare, heterosexual men. If you thought a dude who calls himself a male feminist was a creepy sex pest, wait until you meet the heterosexual male queer. This beta male pussy hound is more cunning than his male feminist counterpart. He's leveled up his game in disarming women. He's the master of the sneak attack. He doesn't just fight for her right to choose and post black squares on Instagram, he's such an ally he's abandoned heteronormative male sexuality altogether, at least according to his dating profiles.

Like the cuttlefish, he's a slink and a trickster. Cuttlefish are cephalopods and thought to be one of the most intelligent creatures in the animal kingdom. They mate in a frenzy. The smaller, weaker male cuttlefish have developed a nasty trick to spread their seed. They masquerade as female cuttlefish, both in appearance through complex camouflage, using chromatophores in their skin, and in demeanor. While the brute, alpha male cuttlefish battle it out for mating rites with the females, the beta cuttlefish creeps into weeds and crevices where the females wait. The females are not threatened, they think he's one of them, and he lingers just long enough to get close and pop some sperm into one of them.

Like being queer, or plus plus, this behavior isn't a sexuality but a courtship strategy. But queer has proved highly useful for the gay agenda, namely as a way to pad out the size of the community in statistics. Recent studies, usually conducted by bloated and worthless gay leftwing nonprofits like the Gay & Lesbian Alliance Against Defamation, or GLAAD, which have long outstayed their welcome, claim 20 percent of people aged eighteen to thirty-four identify as LGBTQ. The Q is what's most important here. It's safe to assume at least three quarters of that group have never had a same-sex encounter and don't plan to, but they'll check Queer on a survey anyway. Simply put, the Q just means à la mode. Like an increasing number of transgenders, it's just fashion.

Microaggressions

A microaggression—the term was coined by a Harvard University psychiatrist—is any casual word, gesture, glance, intonation, or other behavior, intentional or otherwise, that a person perceives as a slight. The offended person is always a Democrat, which is how you know microaggressions aren't real but the province of bored, comfortable people seeking an iota of power in a petty situation. "Tom glanced at me over his computer screen while he was eating a ham sandwich because I'm fat and he wanted to taunt me," might be an example of a microaggression. "I asked Bill how he takes his coffee and he said, 'I like it light and sweet,' and we all knew what he meant by that," might be another.

Microaggressions have nothing to do with the intent of the agent but the perception of the offended. In twenty-first century America, that tends to be how racism works, too. A person makes a choice to be offended or spots casual racism when they've decided they want to seize control over another person or situation, or when they just feel like being noticed. Anyone, except straight white men, have the power to be offended. But like feminism, the microaggression concept has been memed and ridiculed so thoroughly in recent years, it's little more than a punchline. Microaggressions are no more or less absurd than any other fool notion you'll encounter in diversity class. While you're moonlighting as an anonymous troll on Twitter, remember that it is possible for these concepts to be mocked into oblivion, if only one by one, and relentlessly. Let the example of what happened to microaggression be your guide for how to win the information war over Big Diversity.

Unconscious Bias

According to the Office of Diversity and Outreach at the University of California-San Francisco, unconscious biases "are social stereotypes about certain groups of people that individuals form outside their own conscious awareness. Everyone holds unconscious beliefs about various social and identity groups, and these biases stem from one's tendency to organize social worlds by categorizing."

You're likely to hear a lot about unconscious biases in your diversity training. The instruction around this term will imply everyone is racist even if they aren't aware of being a racist. But the term simply means stereotype, and there's nothing unconscious about stereotypes. Stereotypes exist for a reason. One, they tend to hold truths. Without stereotypes, most stand-up comics couldn't have a career. The reality of stereotypes have brought humans together in laughter for centuries. Two, everyone is conscious of them and unless you're a total rube you're aware when a stereotype is influencing your perception of another person or group.

Consider three fictional names—Hugh G. Wang, Bradford Cannington III, and Phelony Jenkins. According to your diversity czar, any impressions you may have about those three people based on their names means you're in for a lifetime of personal inventory and correction. You are part of the problem. But say you find out Hugh G. Wang is a male stripper, Bradford Cannington III is a trailer park dwelling meth addict in West Virginia, and Phelony Jenkins works as a District Attorney. You're probably going to be delightfully surprised that the stereotype didn't hold up. The presence of stereotypes doesn't indicate a society is racist—all societies and groups have them. As a half Filipino, half Native American friend once said to me when stereotyping his own cultures, "stereotypes are like the road signs for society. You shouldn't live by them, but they tend to point you in the right general direction."

White Supremacy

In early 2021, the Coca-Cola corporation was at the center of a conservative media firestorm after an anonymous whistleblower leaked contents of diversity and inclusion training videos offered by LinkedIn Education and utilized by the soft drink giant, according to the *New York Post*. The course was titled "Confronting Racism." One of the slides read, "In the U.S. and other Western nations, white people are socialized to feel that they are inherently superior because they are white." Other slides urged employees to "be less oppressive," "break with white solidarity," and "be less white." The trainings also included video clips of masochistic diversity hustler Robin DiAngelo speaking on her book *White Fragility*; however, DiAngelo denied having anything to do with the course and claims that she did not know she was featured in it.

After the story broke, LinkedIn removed the course from its website. The whistleblower claimed the trainings were mandatory for all Coca-Cola employees. Many other employees corroborate that claim while Coca-Cola executives denied it. "The video circulating on social media is from a publicly available LinkedIn Learning series and is not a focus of our company's curriculum," the company said in a statement. "We will continue to refine this curriculum."

According to critical race scholars, white supremacy is a condition that begins in preschool. Around the time little white babies are ditching the Huggies Pull-Ups for big boy pants they're also learning how the color of their skin makes them superior to other lifeforms putting them first in line for all resources and opportunities the universe has to offer. A switch is flipped, and white babies are summoned to stamp out the black and brown babies, joining their Aryan forefathers to establish the white nation state. Also, around this time, little black and brown babies learn their role of subjugation to the blue-eyed glue-eater with the juice-stained Spiderman T-shirt plotting the destruction of their race as he sticks googly eyes on a paper plate at the next table.

Most people alive today only know white supremacists from movies—caricatures of angry rednecks parading around in white sheets, burning crosses, sporting swastika tattoos. That's because white supremacists don't exist, at least in any remotely significant way. They're on the critically endangered list, and this presented a problem for critical race theorists. As demand for white supremacists has gone through the roof, there just aren't enough of them to go around. The solution must be that if we don't see them, it's because they are literally everywhere, built into every aspect of American society. All white people are white supremacists who benefit from white supremacy, but increasingly plenty of black people are white supremacists, too. Media has grappled with disturbing images of dark-skinned people attending conservative political events by inventing the term "multiracial white supremacy," which refers to any nonwhite person who likes the sound of things like freedom, liberty, capitalism, gun rights, and self-sustainability.

"Don't ever underestimate White supremacy's ability to adapt. The assumption that more racial diversity equals more racial equality is a dangerous myth. Racial diversity can function as a cloaking device, concealing the most powerful forms of White supremacy while giving the appearance of racial progress," CNN producer John Blake wrote in 2021, calling white supremacy "elastic [...] like taffy." "It will still be White supremacy, with a tan."

Reporting from a pro-Trump rally in 2018 featuring "dozens" of black, Latino, and Asian people, the *Daily Beast*'s Arun Gupta asked, "Is the future of hate multicultural?"

"By bringing diversity to what is at heart a white-supremacist movement, people of color give it legitimacy to challenge state power and commit violence against their enemies," he wrote, adding "libertarianism is another gateway" for people of color to find themselves on the "far right."

"A lot of these young guys [...] who are being sucked into white nationalism, start out being worked up about Ayn Rand in high school," an author quoted in the article says.

In January 2021, under the headline "To understand Trump's support, we must think in terms of multiracial Whiteness," New York University associate professor Cristina Beltran wrote in the *Washington Post*, "Multiracial whiteness reflects an understanding of whiteness as a political color and not simply a racial identity—a discriminatory worldview in which feelings of freedom and belonging are produced through the persecution and dehumanization of others."

"For voters who see the very act of acknowledging one's racial identity as itself racist, the politics of multiracial whiteness reinforces their desired approach to colorblind individualism. In the politics of multiracial whiteness, anyone can join the MAGA movement and engage in the wild freedom of unbridled rage and conspiracy theories."

Chapter Four

Pink Shirt Day on the Rig:
Tales from the Diversity Dystopia in
Business and Industry

When he was a youngster Jeremy S. had humble ambitions. "My goal was to be on unemployment. That's sort of the Newfoundland way of life," he says. "The former conservative Prime Minister once said Atlantic Canada has a culture of defeat, which I don't think is incorrect."

One night in a bar he heard about an opportunity that seemed to suit him, prospecting for oil in western Canada. "Since the fishing industry collapsed, Newfoundlanders have historically gone out to Alberta for work. So, I figured, why not?"

For many winters in the 2000s, Jeremy, who asked me to use a pseudonym because he feared retaliation from his employer, earned a living riding a four-wheeler through the forests laying sticks of dynamite in the ground and seeing what came up. "We'd just walk through the woods in minus forty degrees, thirteen hours a day, laying a grid of cables, setting off explosions, and then through the explosions we could sort of tell what's underneath the ground. It was seasonal work. In the spring the ground became muddy, and they'd lay you off."

"I was a leftist back then," he says. But as he got older and his priorities evolved, Jeremy pursued stable employment within the oil industry. About ten years ago he ended up on a drilling rig.

His first day on the job he recalls being taunted by a female cook and another man who worked in the galley. "All day long they were just saying, 'We're going to make you one of us,' and I was like 'Shit, man, that doesn't sound good.'"

At the end of the shift, after he unpacked his belongings in his shared room on the rig, the man pinned his arms back and the female cook began punching him in the chest and stomach.

"She was just giving me body shots. And then they made me sniff Percocet so that it would be in my bloodstream, and I couldn't tell on them, because we were subject to possible blood tests," he says.

"It's more of a harsher crowd on drilling rigs, more like a prison vibe in terms of roughness."

Jeremy eventually moved to a production rig, where he now works about one hundred miles off the coast of Newfoundland in three-week-long shifts.

"I'd say the workforce is about 90 percent white male," he tells me on a video call from his dormitory. "We just had Pink Shirt Day on the rig."

"Excuse me?" I asked.

"Maybe it's a Canadian thing. I think it started in the schools. You're supposed to wear a pink shirt to show you're against bullying, or something."

"Did anyone wear a pink shirt?" I asked.

"Yeah, the rig boss had one on. And they were handing out pink shirts for people to wear, and some put it on. And they had little pink disposable face masks for everyone to wear, too. I'm not really sure how effective it is."

One of the pink shirts, which reads "IT'S COOL 2B KIND" with a pair of sunglasses for the Os in "cool," was then placed in a glass case, like a jersey from a winning sports team, and displayed in a hallway.

Jeremy shows me a poster, "Random Acts of Kindness. How can we uplift those around us on a daily basis?" it reads, with a pink rocket blasting off in the center surrounded by white space. Alongside the phallic graphic, employees signed their names and left a note about what Pink Shirt Day meant to them.

"Always be kind to people," one wrote.

"It costs nothing to be kind," said another.

"Keep it in mind to always be kind," scribbled a third.

"Be kind to everyone," an employee named Rocky wrote.

"Be kind to all kinds of people," wrote a man who signed his name Blake.

I was sensing a lack of enthusiasm.

Before Pink Shirt Day, employees signed an "inclusion pledge." "Inclusion Pledge: I pledge to be inclusive," a poster in another hallway reads in bold font surrounded by the signatures of the rig workers.

Jeremy, like the other workers, is required to attend a meeting at the start of each three-week shift where various corporate initiatives are discussed. Each session includes a lesson on diversity and inclusion.

During one training, an animated Pixar short called *Purl* was shown to the oil rig workers. Purl is a goofy, gender-ambiguous, walking, talking pink ball of yarn starting her first day on the job at a venture capital firm called B.R.O. (get it?). Only fit, young, well-tailored white men work at B.R.O. Eager but nervous Purl steps off the elevator with her box of desktop knickknacks to be met with confused and disapproving glances from the bros at B.R.O. As the day goes on, Purl is having a hard time fitting in. The guys aren't laughing at her stupid quips, won't let her speak in meetings, and don't invite her to join them for happy hour.

To combat this, Purl tries reinvention. She knits a suit for herself, slams her fists on the table, and barks about profits; she tells bawdy jokes at the water cooler. Now she's one of the guys and the bros suddenly adore Purl. Then another ball of yarn, this one yellow and named Lacey, comes into the office. Lacey is as docile and naïve as Purl once was and Purl feels bad, remembering her former self, as she yuks it up with her new friends, the bros. Purl invites Lacey to join her and the bros, and the bros are forced to accept Lacey because they now respect Purl and Purl invited her. The next time we see the office, it's full of anthropomorphic balls of yarn, Purl is back to her old sweet self, and everyone is getting along better than ever.

Watching it, I thought, even if Purl weren't a ball of yarn, I wouldn't want to work alongside her either. She's puerile, annoying, and desperate for validation. How'd she get a job here in the first place? She didn't even think to wear a suit on her first day. In fact, considering she only later put on clothes, she arrived naked. More strangely, it becomes clear Purl isn't treated negatively because she looks different or is female, but because she's bumbling, amateurish, and too soft-natured for such a demanding environment. It's clear the bros aren't bigots. Purl just doesn't fit into the culture of that workplace, one established long before she arrived. So, what's the problem here? What message are a bunch of guys on an oil rig in the middle of the Atlantic Ocean to take away?

The message is clear: there's something wrong with them, not Purl. White male work culture, if there is such a thing, is aggressive, exclusionary, and boneheaded but by no means superior or beyond redemption, the film would have the rig workers believe. If you act like the bros, you will be embraced, but is that what anyone really wants? No, what the office needs is one courageous, entitled ball of yarn to realize it is her duty to suck the testosterone from the room for the betterment of all.

The 2019 short was the directorial debut of a woman named Kristen Lester and by early 2021 had been viewed over twenty-one million times on YouTube. (Less than two years after her first whack at directing, Lester holds the impressive title of Head of Story at Pixar Animation Studios. Considering everything seemed to be going just fine at B.R.O. before Purl the gender disrupter rolled herself off the elevator, I wondered how things must be going for the male employees at Pixar now, if there are even any left).

"You see these 'diversity' signs all around the workplace," Jeremy tells me.

One poster he shows me nags employees about locker-room talk. There's a stock photo of a skittish female in a hardhat surrounded by imposing male colleagues. "The message: 'They're just jokes. Don't be so sensitive,'" it reads. "Locker-room talk can be damaging to both men and women. It primes men to think of women as sexual objects, and forces men to discard decency and feelings in order to fit in."

"Shift the conversation," the poster instructs. "Question respectfully: What do you mean by that? Share your feelings: I don't like when you make those kinds of jokes. Be an ally."

"The message: Why is he taking parental leave? Doesn't he care about his job?" another poster reads. "Reinforcing stereotypical gender norms by calling masculinity and job commitment into question can make men feel ashamed and lead to disengagement. Set an example, support men who take parental leave."

"These young people don't want to work, they're always on Facebook and Twitter!" exclaims another poster Jeremy shows me. "Millennials represent almost half the world's workforce. Microbreaks—such as checking a social media page—can lead to workers feeling more refreshed and efficient." It advises young people on the job to defend their social media habit by proclaiming, "I think it is positive that I am able to use technology to refresh myself."

At a recent diversity meeting Jeremy says the presenter, someone from the home offices in Alberta, displayed a slide with bullet points describing how the company is actively seeking "diverse" applicants for open positions.

"With a reduced crew because of COVID, there were only white men at that particular diversity meeting. So, the message seemed to be, 'We don't want people like you,'" Jeremy says. "Which isn't that uplifting."

In addition to diversity lectures at the beginning of each three-week long shift, employees are encouraged to attend periodic, more intensive seminars. The company offers free lunch and double-time pay for workers who sign up for an all-day course, which may involve traveling 2,200 miles from Newfoundland to Edmonton.

For decades having a good safety record, beginning with workers in the field, meant life or death for an oil company. Governments used that to award contracts and land-leasing permits. But that focus began to shift and now workplace training hours are split between safety and another profit lifeline, diversity-signaling to liberal governments who have fossil fuels in their crosshairs.

One time, Jeremy says, the crew was given T-shirts with the company logo in rainbow gay pride colors and was handed rainbow rubber bracelets. They posed for a group picture wearing the rainbow shirts, but no one is quite sure why or what happened to the picture.

Scout around the Internet, or attend any Pride parade, and you'll see that gay clubs are actively encouraged at oil companies. ExxonMobil, for one, has an employee PRIDE network with chapters in six countries. Shell Oil's main Diversity and Inclusive website prominently displays a rainbow Shell logo at the top, suggesting there's an LGBT priority in the company's definition of Diversity and Inclusion. Shell Canada's website features an additional page, "Supporting our LGBT Talent at Shell," that proclaims: "At Shell, we care about the diversity of our people because we believe that a fully inclusive workplace allows our employees to flourish and so allows our business to flourish. When our employees excel, we excel. It's for this reason that we are proud to support our lesbian, gay, bisexual, and transgender (LGBT) staff, promoting equality for employees regardless of sexual orientation or gender identity."

The Canadian site also profiles LGBT workers, including a man named James Fowler, who founded an LGBT club at Shell Australia called Kaleidoscope. Fowler describes being once closeted on the job because he "wanted to be judged on performance and skills and was determined not to be known as 'the gay engineer.'" He then cites a statistic without a source, that "Employees who are 'out' at work are 30% more productive than those who aren't."

"We live in a very heteronormative society, where not everybody understands what is meant by gender-neutral or gender-inclusive language. Educating a workforce about unconscious biases and various kinds of diversity raises awareness. Training people to use gender-neutral terms such as 'partner' rather than 'boyfriend/girlfriend' or informing them about the terms *cisgender* and *transgender* can go a long way in fostering an inclusive environment," Fowler says on the site.

With an estimated 171 billion barrels, Canada has 10 percent of the world's known oil reserves, the third most oil of any country. The Member of Parliament representing Newfoundland and Labrador, Canada's hub for offshore drilling, is Seamus O'Regan of the Liberal Party. He's also Canada's Minister of Natural Resources—the guy in charge of the government contracts and pipelines—and he's openly gay.

Sexuality is a pretty big deal for O'Regan. In 2017, he addressed the Canadian House of Commons about it, describing a lifelong personal struggle that drove him to alcoholism. He didn't come out as gay until his late 30s. "This is about shame," he said. "Being made to feel shame for being different. Growing up terrified of being ostracized, growing up, keeping some of the most beautiful, intimate parts of your life a secret, wondering if there was something twisted in you."

I wondered if it was too cynical to believe hundreds of hours of diversity training, even forcing workers to pose for a photo in rainbow T-shirts, was all done to make one gay resources minister feel loved. Then again, it's not so far-fetched. Talking to Jeremy it was clear the rig's diversity initiatives were not only seen as boring and stupid by the workers but also completely unnecessary.

"For years, the single focus on the rig was safety. Now, the diversity officers always tell us diversity makes us safer, but they never explain how," Jeremy says. "They try to link this back to safety, our number one goal of safety, and diversity makes us safer."

It's simple how diversity makes the company safer, if you realize they're not referring to spills and explosions. But two thousand miles away from the boardroom, in the middle of the Atlantic, this nagging has only made workers feel less valued.

"The cumulative effect of all this niceness, never-of-fend-anyone culture, is infantilizing. It feels like kindergarten," Jeremy says. "I worked three jobs with all women. They were just as crude as the guys. At no point did I try to weaponize their sexism."

There are virtually no black people living in Newfoundland and Labrador, where most of the rig workers live and the population is nearly 90 percent white. The rest are mostly aboriginal.

"I don't think corporate understands the goal of this diversity training. It's a dog whistle for basically being anti-white. It's not about getting along more; it's about overthrowing the existing system. I'm all for, 'Don't judge people for being different' and 'Try to get along.' It doesn't seem to be building more camaraderie, even though that's what they think the goal is. When you see it in practice, you see people get radicalized by the notion of 'diversity.'"

"There was one black person in my town," he recalls. "And he was an inmate in the penitentiary up the street. But I'd still sometimes see these 'Black Lives Matter' signs in windows. They're now saying black people built the nation of Canada. I think by the 1970s there were, like, maybe thirty thousand black people in all of Canada. What are they even talking about?"

"At the end of the day, guys will still be guys just never when corporate is around. When I shaved off my beard my boss said to me, 'must be trying to get the smell of cock off you,'" Jeremy laughs. "That was a pretty good burn, I admit."

During the months after I met Jeremy, I talked to dozens of everyday people in the private sector willing to share stories about the time they were sent to diversity training for their job. The conversations usually began the same. *I'm not sure why you're interested in this*, they'd say. *It's boring.* But after an hour or so of talking, workers across the economy found themselves increasingly incensed, or just amused, recounting what they'd been subjected to. Seminars that at first seemed like a waste of time were now looking, at best, passive aggressive and condescending. In other cases, they were downright hateful. From bankers to shop girls and engineers to office managers, diversity training had snuck into every area of business in the U.S., and it appeared only to be getting worse. Another theme I picked up on was that resistance to your company's diversity czar was not only futile but also dangerous.

After the George Floyd riots that swept the nation's large cities in 2020, workers everywhere noticed their companies injecting headlines into the workplace and, it seemed, assuring everyone their employer followed a certain side of the story. Companywide memos, sometimes to tens of thousands of employees across the world, went out from human resources departments and CEOs offering emotional support in the wake of Floyd's death and the social unrest that followed. Often in the most innocuous and unsubstantive way possible, they reaffirmed a strong commitment to diversity and, in doing so, tacitly condemned that sneaking nondiverse element, whatever that may be, should anyone be concerned.

Who are they even talking to? I wondered reading some of these memos forwarded to me, bloodless dictums rattled off into a void. I imagined an Alexa device floating through the clouds of Neptune answering questions about race that no one asked. While I haven't spent much time in the corporate world, I imagined this is how most communications sounded: aggressively insipid and judicious, something for the files in case the lawyers ever needed it. But here we were talking about the most charged political issue of the day, and a framework already had been in place at nearly every company in the nation, establishing a culture of reverence for "diversity," which, while most may not have realized it at first, was just another word for "race," specifically all races except one. The once innocuous notion of diversity was now inseparable from politics and its weaponization as an amorphous, emotional tool was inarguably synonymous with one, dominant side of the political spectrum: the left. In the workplace, that meant people who'd not given it much thought in the past were getting increasingly agitated.

While normal people don't think too much about the skin color of the person one cubicle over, corporate seemed to think diversity was something enigmatic that might be making people leery. It was as though diversity were some sort of strange, ominous, and concerning object that just appeared next to the water cooler, like one of those monoliths from *2001: A Space Odyssey*. Someone decided it needed to be not only addressed but interpreted repeatedly, especially when issues of racial strife appeared in the news.

Unlike other office fixtures, like a new copy machine, diversity's purpose is never quite explained beyond being a specter of innate, unexplainable goodness. Diversity is not surmountable and there is no instruction manual. Using political philosophies developed in academia but tamped down for the office, diversity is presented as a journey without a destination. *We're not there yet*, the emails often intoned, *we may never get there, but we are committed to striving to ensure safety and diversity.*

"Ok, here we go," Steve, a retail worker in Tennessee says, pulling up one of countless emails from Ralph Lauren's Manager of Diversity and Inclusion, Global People and Development. "You can see here he has his pronouns listed in his email signature."

This one is from January. "RL's statement on the D.C. insurrection," it reads.

"Actions and resources following yesterday's events in Washington, D.C. We will only win by doing the right thing and caring. We must keep dignity, quality and maintain sensitivity in all that we do. That is what this company is about. We care about our own and we will do the right thing and stay true to who we are as well."

The email then featured company leaders reflecting on the incident and referred workers to the "mental health support team," insinuating anyone punching a clock to sell jeans on a Saturday must be as grief stricken as Don Lemon or Rachel Maddow.

Several months before that, Steve, who also asked I not use his real name because he's afraid of getting fired, took his first hour-and-a-half diversity and inclusion training seminar, something he'd been putting off and nearly forgot about. As with many workplaces, employees at Ralph Lauren are required to attend the seminar at some point during their employment, but there's no real time frame for when it must be completed. For Steve, it sat on his to-do list for about three years. How he ever managed to process all the diversity around him during that time without attending the seminar is anyone's guess.

One morning he decided to finally get it out of the way. This one was a teleconference with five other employees from across the country, all retail floor workers. It was led by a man Steve had never seen before, and he wasn't sure how he was affiliated with the company, if at all.

"It was a black dude with dreadlocks, of course," Steve says. "He was very nice and friendly but just seemed like one of those, you know, professors you had who was just so progressive that it was almost boring. Not at all interesting or controversial, but I guess that's how you have to be. This is a corporate presentation in a corporate setting."

Steve mostly tuned it out. He turned the camera and microphone off on his laptop and was doing other things as the seminar droned on.

"It felt like preschool. It was so patronizing," he says. "It was, like, saying if you're in a conversation with a black person, you have to keep these things in mind. A lot of the gist was how to approach people who are in nonprivileged positions. People who are in privileged positions should be more attentive and listening and really wait to say anything. But they never defined what a privileged position was, it was just assumed that you would know what they meant."

The other retail workers attending the seminar were all women. "And they all talked in that annoying upspeak way, where everything is a question? And they chimed in about ways to check their privilege? And realizing they come from some places of privilege? And that they are more privileged than maybe other employees would be?" Steve said, mockingly.

He said everything was quite predictable and innocuous, considering this stuff is already relentlessly drilled into the American psyche from all angles...until an image came up on the screen that shocked Steve.

"I was triggered," he admits. The image was an animation of a group of people on one side holding a Confederate flag and another group of people opposite who were looking at the flag. The people looking at the flag had peculiar expressions on their faces. The instructor asked, "What do you think is going on in the life of these people?" he asked about the flag holders. "How do the people looking at this flag feel about it?"

"It just got really weird from there," Steve says. He could no longer keep quiet and turned on his microphone. "What if the people who are holding the flag feel offended by the people who are judging them, because this is their culture and their own and nothing else, isn't that all? Can't they be offended, too?"

Things went downhill quick.

"I can see why you might say that," the diversity ambassador said to Steve, but Steve wasn't finished.

"I was, like, 'Wait, why can't we just be adults if we're having a disagreement in the workplace? Why do we have to hear all these sensitivity rules about people's feelings? Like, of course, we're going to take the time and listen to what he or she has said, but I'm not going to treat them as if they're a small child,'" Steve blurted out.

There was a weighty silence as the instructor again collected himself. "Well, Steve, that's one way to look at it. But at the same time, remember we have to be sensitive with people and people's feelings and how they deal with stuff."

Steve shot back. "Yeah, that's fair and all, but this is a workplace. We're not here to be kind to each other, we're here to run a business."

"At that point, I think he recognized that, 'All right, this guy is not going to go along with any of this,' and he moved on," Steve says. Steve then remembered a bizarre incident from about two years ago. It was July Fourth and Steve was scrolling through social media when he came across a post from a photographer he admired at the time. It was an image of an upside-down American flag.

"In the caption of the photo this guy was saying, 'I immigrated here twenty years ago from Switzerland,' or wherever, 'and I'm really unhappy to even say that I live in America. America treats immigrants so badly here,' blah blah blah blah. And he was, like, 'Remember at your barbecues and while you're grilling and drinking who cleans your houses and who cleans your cars? Who cleans your hotels?' So, I went off on this guy," Steve recalls.

"Are you saying all Hispanic people are good for is menial labor? Is that what you think of Hispanic people?" he asked in the comments section. There was a heated back and forth before Steve dropped it and went on with his day.

"The next day, three of my immediate managers emailed me and were, like, did you say something to this guy? I didn't know what they were talking about. I'd forgot about it by then." The managers told Steve his exchange with the photographer was making rounds around the company. The man was apparently well-connected at Ralph Lauren, unbeknownst to Steve at the time, who had listed his place of work in his social media profile. "They said Ralph Lauren himself knew about it," Steve says.

"I was nearly fired, but I was the one defending Hispanics. I was standing up for 'diversity,'" he says. He decided the diversity class should hear this story, but the instructor coolly batted it away.

"You have to think about where this other guy was coming from," the instructor told him.

"But the other guy doesn't even work for the company!" Steve protested. "I was explaining my thoughts freely on the internet, so I don't understand how something like this could come back and I'm not treated with kid gloves, but other people would be."

That paid hour of free time, as Steve first saw it, suddenly took on a more sinister light. "It felt like I was a kid who had to be, like, you know, retrained. I mean, that's what it is. It's trying to rewire your brain to be alert to all the 'woke.'"

Michael works for a Northwestern Mutual contractor near Los Angeles. Being openly homosexual, Michael was invited to join an LGBTQ+ diversity and inclusion initiative through his company.

"I know that the insurance industry tends to be more conservative, but I work with plenty of gay people. There's never any issues. I didn't think this was something that was needed, but I decided to join anyway," he told me.

Michael, not his real name, was flown to Northwestern Mutual's headquarters in Milwaukee for a weekend retreat about the gays. "We're sitting in the top floor conference room of this skyscraper, this is where the C-suite board would be for corporate, and we sit in this room for five hours talking about, *what is gay culture, who are these people, what are they like?*" Then, "in walks this high-end lesbian financial advisor," Michael says. The woman was overweight, stout, in her thirties, with short hair. "She tells us she's the daughter of a pastor, so I'm automatically thinking she's resentful toward Christians. Since then, I found out she's transgender now and identifies as a man," Michael scoffs. "Of course."

Drawing on her experience in the company, the lesbian spoke to the group about what it's like selling insurance products to gay men. "And she just painted us all as these alcoholic whores. She said, 'Whenever I budget for a single gay man or a gay couple, I always put a line item in for boys and toys.' She literally said that. I almost lost it on her. It all actually felt really homophobic. I was thinking, there are plenty of gay men who are sober, who've had horrible times with alcohol and drugs—that's very prevalent in our community—we're not whores, we don't want to sleep around, we want to get married, we want kids."

Michael kept his mouth shut. Everyone else seemed intrigued by the lesbian's presentation, nodding along and taking notes about the gay party circuit. Michael soon realized he was the only conservatively minded person in the room.

"As the weekend went on, I noticed I was being boxed out of the group because I was getting a reputation for challenging the group's assumptions. They were all about the intersection of race and gender and sexuality. They wouldn't look me in the eye, or they would glare at me whenever I brought up the diversity of opinion found in the gay community. They didn't like that. They pushed against it. They were developing this kind of *Mean Girls* mentality. The whole thing ended up being about trashing conservatives and Trump and less about gay equality."

Despite this, Michael returned to Los Angeles and joined his company's LGBT diversity board, believing he could make a difference by providing an alternative perspective to their monolithic, intersectional depiction of the homosexual agenda. He lasted about a year and a half. "But the board went from liberal to *woke* overnight," Michael recalls. Every meeting pitted him against the rest of the board. Tensions only worsened as the 2020 presidential election loomed. Members took to monitoring his social media activity. "Once I posted something about Tulsi Gabbard and protecting women's sports, and they came for me over that."

The hatred and stubbornness became too much for Michael to bear, and instead of compromising his beliefs or being whipped into silence, he stepped down. "I decided I'm done with this shit because I can't fight it. All I'm going to do is make them hate me and that might reflect very badly on my boss, who is prominent in the company. I went to the leader of the group and I said, 'I can't sit on this board anymore and I'm not comfortable; and with the election coming up, it's only going to get worse and I'm not going to back off from what I believe. At the same time, I'm not going to make all these meetings horrific for you.'"

The experience left him with a sense of surrender. "I was like, OK, this is what corporations are doing now. This is how they're acting. They don't actually want a conversation. They don't want to have any sort of difference of opinion. They want submission."

He suspects the most senior executives in his company all vote Republican, "I guarantee it," but down the ladder other forces are in control. "I see two main issues here where all this wokeness is infecting companies. People don't want to be looked at as insensitive, bigoted, racist, or homophobic—they're deathly afraid of getting canceled, they're deathly afraid of bad press. That's part of it. And also they'd rather capitulate to these people to make them shut up rather than actually push back on them. They don't want to hear it from these annoying, woke social justice warriors. So they just go along with it."

Sam, who works for a large bank in St. Louis, swears he found a hired narc in one of his diversity sessions—someone planted to intimidate workers and gauge their responses. Years before the random berating black woman appeared in a teleconference to blame his IT department for the death of George Floyd, Sam attended a five-day training week in Charlotte, North Carolina, with a colleague. A prickly woman in the diversity and inclusion seminar had been making everyone squirm all morning. "She was offended by anything that anyone said to her. She was offended by the leader, offended by anything anyone said in the group," Sam recalled.

The woman told a story about a successful project she oversaw that received accolades from the upper echelon of the company. "My colleague paid her a compliment on her work; it was very diplomatic, and she was offended by that! She said he was speaking down to her because she was a woman, and he was a man." After the woman left and the session ended, Sam's colleague—who Sam described as, "the nicest guy, totally on board with all things diversity and inclusion"—was flummoxed. He didn't understand what set off this woman. No matter what he said, she had it out for him. Sam thought the whole display not only strange, but completely over the top. "I told him, I thought it was an act. I think this woman was an actor who was plugged in there to make everybody feel like no matter what you say or do, someone's going to get offended at all times. That's what's dangerous about all this stuff to me."

Chapter Five

Forget the Alamo:
The Pussification of the U.S. Military

On February 3, 2021, Secretary of Defense Lloyd J. Austin III ordered a sixty-day standdown across the entire Department of Defense to root out what he called "extremism" in the U.S. military. Speaking to reporters, Pentagon Press Secretary John Kirby explained the directive. While extremism in the military is "not a significant problem," it still "has to be addressed."

Even a small amount of extremism is too much, the Pentagon said. "The vast majority of men and women who serve in uniform and the military are doing so with honor, integrity, and character, and do not espouse the sorts of beliefs that lead to the kind of conduct that can be so detrimental to good order and discipline and in fact is criminal," Kirby told reporters.

"It's got to be a leadership issue down to the lowest levels, small unit leadership all the way up to him," he continued, referring to Secretary Austin. "So, if you consider it a leadership issue, then maybe there will be some potential solutions there to allow us greater visibility."

It was two weeks into Joe Biden's presidency and less than a month after what the media had dubbed the

Trump insurrection. On January 6, 2021, tens of thousands of Americans amassed in Washington, D.C. where three separate rallies converged, billed as the March for Trump, the Save America Rally, and Stop the Steal. Grassroots organizers called the gatherings First Amendment events intended to "demand transparency and protect election integrity" on the same day Congress was to officially approve the 2020 election results.

In the late morning, President Trump addressed supporters at the Ellipse. A march to the U.S. Capitol Building already was planned for that afternoon. "We're going to walk down to the Capitol, and we're going to cheer on our brave senators and congressmen and women," the president told the crowd. "I know that everyone here will soon be marching over to the Capitol building to peacefully and patriotically make your voices heard," he said. "Our exciting adventures and boldest endeavors have not yet begun. My fellow Americans, for our movement, for our children, and for our beloved country…And I say this despite all that's happened. The best is yet to come."

The standdown followed a report from National Public Radio revealing some people involved in the events at the U.S. Capitol were either active-duty military or retired veterans. The government-funded broadcaster compiled a list of individuals facing charges either federally or in the District of Columbia and found of the more than 140 people charged at that time, a review of military records, social media accounts, court documents, and news reports indicated at least twenty-seven individuals had served or were currently enlisted in the military.

The headlines went ballistic: nearly 20 percent of "insurrectionists" were U.S. military. In the minds of many mainstream news consumers, thousands of people violently stormed the Capitol that day with an intent to overthrow the U.S. government. In reality, a few hundred carried-away lollygaggers wandered aimlessly and snapped selfies once they got inside. Someone stole a lectern. Someone else propped his feet up on Nancy Pelosi's desk. Also contrary to reports, only one person was killed that day: an unarmed, female Trump supporter named Ashli Babbitt, shot by law enforcement as a mob tried to break into a side entrance of the Capitol. The officer who killed her was spared any punitive action and his identity was covered up for months.

To further its case, in the report NPR quoted a 2019 survey conducted by *Military Times* magazine and Syracuse University's Institute for Veterans and Military Families. "Roughly one-third of active-duty troops said they had 'personally witnessed examples of white nationalism or ideo-logical-driven racism within the ranks in recent months,'" the report claimed. "Troops said they had seen 'swastikas being drawn on service members' cars, tattoos affiliated with white supremacist groups, stickers supporting the Ku Klux Klan and Nazi-style salutes between individuals.'"

That was an outrageous statistic that would give any rational person pause. Of the nearly 2.5 million active and reserve service members in 2019, the study surveyed 1,630 individuals who were all subscribers to *Military Times* magazine. The magazine had come under fire by conser-vatives for veering into never-Trump partisanship in recent years. *Military Times* headlines during Trump's presidency included, "There's a movement building to reverse DoD's policy on LGBTQ pride flag and other banners," "Report: Trump disparaged US war dead as 'losers,' 'suckers'," "Trump's misleading claims on military readiness and veteran care," "Trump's popularity slips in latest *Military Times* poll," and "Former military leaders: Trump's tweet is 'attack on our electoral process.'"

The survey questions were highly suspect. "Have you personally witnessed examples of white nationalism or racism within the ranks of the military?" one asked, lumping white nationalism in with a general interpretation of racism. It was unclear what a "Nazi-style salute" might be. The mention of "tattoos affiliated with white supremacist groups" was also questionable. In 2018, a fact-checker for the *New Yorker* magazine was fired after she mistook a Marine veteran's tattoo for the Nazis' Iron Cross. It turned out to be a "Titan 2" symbol for the platoon he served in in Afghanistan. And it was anyone's guess what a sticker supporting the Ku Klux Klan might look like and to what extent any such symbolism was merely Confederate flag paraphernalia—arguably not a racist symbol in the minds of many Southerners.

The report also ignored all existing Department of Defense regulations against participation in extremist groups and bans on gang affiliations and insignias. "Service members must reject active participation in organizations that advance supremacist or extremist ideology, which includes those that advance, encourage, or advocate illegal discrimination based on race, creed, color, sex, religion, ethnicity, or national origin, or those that advance, encourage, or advocate the use of force, violence, or criminal activity or otherwise advance efforts to deprive individuals of their civil rights," the regulations state.

The department has long warned about recruitment efforts from extremist groups that would value the knowledge and training military personnel undergo. "Active participation" in such groups is strictly prohibited. "Active participation includes, but is not limited to: 'Fundraising, demonstrating, rallying, recruiting, training, organizing, leading members, distributing material (including posting online), or knowingly wearing gang colors or clothing, having tattoos or body markings associated with such gangs or organizations; or otherwise engaging in activities in furtherance of objectives of such gangs or organizations that are detrimental to good order, discipline, or mission accomplishment or are incompatible with military service,'" the regulations state.

None of that mattered to the media or the Biden administration. After Biden's inauguration, the nation's capital was enveloped in an authoritarian gloom. Barriers were erected around the Capitol building and National Guard troops patrolled the windswept streets of downtown Washington. The city belonging to the American people had been closed off under military force as the newly installed president settled in under what many considered to be dubious circumstances.

The Capitol breach, followed by the NPR report, provided the perfect catalyst for the new president's administration to conduct an ideological purge of the armed forces as he presided over a capitol city that looked, from the outside, like it had just undergone a military coup.

Under Biden's direction, the Department of Defense disseminated anti-extremism training materials to leaders in all branches of the military. The intention was to propagate the new administration's definition as extremism, as well as to train leadership and servicemembers to recognize and report people with certain beliefs in their ranks.

Reporting, the Department of Defense stressed, was mandatory. "If you observe a coworker exhibiting concerning behaviors, you have a responsibility to report it through the chain of command or supervision to your local security manager, and/or directly to the Insider Threat program office. Report issues of imminent threats or activity that may constitute criminal conduct to local law enforcement immediately," the materials read.

The definition of extremism, however, centered only on grossly overblown media fictions about one side of the political spectrum while ignoring, and even at times celebrating, the other side's radicals. In March 2021, U.S. Navy training slides on extremism leaked to Fox News told recruits they were permitted to openly support Black Lives Matter at work but were forbidden from discussing other "politically partisan issues."

When asked by a reporter whether discussing Black Lives Matter at work is considered partisan, Kirby responded that he was unwilling to answer that question. To do so, he said, would be to "go down a rabbit hole on a million different things."

The 2009 massacre at Fort Hood in Texas, in which a U.S. Army major radicalized by Islamism killed thirteen and wounded thirty others, was a distant memory. So was the more recent December 2019 terrorist attack by a Saudi Air Force officer training at a Navy base in Pensacola, Florida, which left three U.S. sailors dead and eight others wounded. Or the 2015 shooting at a Navy and Marine reserve center in Chattanooga, Tennessee, that left four marines and a sailor dead at the hands of Kuwait-born Muhammad Youssef Abdulazeez.

That wasn't the sort of workplace extremism that concerned Biden's Department of Defense. White supremacy was the new internal threat, despite such people barely existing in the civilian population, let alone the military. To justify the conservative "witch hunt," as servicemembers described it to me, the Department of Defense cited Supreme Court precedence involving First Amendment rights and military service.

"Although Service members enjoy the right to free speech protected by the First Amendment, the unique character of the military community and of the military mission requires a balancing of those rights with the important purpose of the military," the Department published on its website alongside a thirteen-page training document.

"In fact, the Supreme Court of the United States noted as follows: '[t]his Court has long recognized that the military is, by necessity, a specialized society separate from civilian society. We have also recognized that the military has, again by necessity, developed laws and traditions of its own during its long history." The differences between the military and civilian communities result from the fact that "it is the primary business of armies and navies to fight or be ready to fight wars should the occasion arise... [w]hile the members of the military are not excluded from the protection granted by the First Amendment, the different character of the military community and of the military mission requires a different application of those protections. The fundamental necessity for obedience, and the consequent necessity for imposition of discipline, may render permissible within the military that which would be constitutionally impermissible outside it."

There was some irony in Biden's Department of Defense quoting that Supreme Court decision. It's from *Parker v. Levy*. In 1974, a white Army captain stationed at a U.S. Army hospital in South Carolina, Dr. Howard Levy, urged black enlisted men to refuse to serve in Vietnam because "they are discriminated against and denied their freedom in the United States, and ...discriminated against in Vietnam by being given all the hazardous duty and they are suffering the majority of casualties." The Court ruled against Levy, holding that the First Amendment can be applied differently in the military context. It is, by today's standards, very antiwoke but now being used to justify the military's progressive ideological overhaul.

The only examples of extremism mentioned in the training documents relate to white nationalists, neo-Nazis, and neo-fascists. The events in Washington, D.C., on January 6 were also mentioned but nothing of the year-long rioting and destruction from far-left radicals in major cities. Military leaders were provided with a series of antic-ipated questions and sample answers, like a script, for how to respond to concerns from enlistees.

Q: If there have been issues with extremism inside the Department of Defense for a long time, why is the Secretary of Defense so focused on this now?

A: The increased level of domestic protests around the country in the past several months has emboldened some violent extremist groups to take more aggressive anti-government and racially motivated actions. These groups are known to actively target current and former military personnel. In light of current events, the Secretary wants DoD personnel at all levels to understand the threat and be trained and educated to take appropriate actions when they see indicators of extremism.

Q: Does DoD actually have a problem with extremist groups?

A: We are seeing an increase in concerning behavior. We believe this is based on societal increases, but there's also an increase in the reporting of suspect behavior. We are actively tracking down these leads and identifying any other associations with these sorts of groups. That's why we need all DoD personnel to report concerning behaviors appropriately so we can thoroughly review all credible reports.

Q: Does DoD check the social media records of Service members, DoD civilian employees, and prospective recruits?

A: Consent for obtaining publicly available social media information is provided when Service members and DoD civilian employees submit their Personnel Security Questionnaire (SF-86) to initiate the background investigation process. DoD is examining a scalable means of implementing social media screening in conjunction with background investigations. Furthermore, the FBI currently screens social media for extremism and criminal activity.

After Biden's directive, Devin, an officer in the United States Air Force stationed in North Carolina, noticed work becoming more tense. He asked me to use an alias to avoid backlash on the job.

"I work with fighter pilots, we're a pretty diverse bunch. It's not a very PC environment. We can get raunchy," he tells me. Airmen living at dorms on base were members of an online message board. They initially used the board to share memes, "making fun of leadership, other officers, senior NCOs. It was actually in good taste," or to post about starting clubs on the base or hosting a movie night. Politics never came up.

But "[i]t shifted from that. Tensions started getting really high. It went from a lighthearted, fun club to, 'Breonna Taylor was murdered by police because she was a black woman.' They started lifting up all these examples. It was pretty morbid."

Someone on the message board then created a counter for how many days had passed since a "nonviolent black person is killed by police unjustly."

"Like how some workplaces have a counter for how many days since the last accident at work, it was like that," Devin says.

"It shouldn't be in the workplace because it's so sensitive right now. Some of it was just literally putting up there on the board the names of black and brown people that were killed in the last year, painting them as this totally innocent person. Now we're tippy toeing to make sure we don't offend somebody by saying, like, 'hey, do you actually look into what the police report said?'"

Promoting, campaigning for, or criticizing any political candidate, and especially the Commander-in-Chief, is highly frowned upon in the military, and possibly illegal depending on rank. While the Hatch Act was designed to protect federal employees from political coercion in the workplace, the pervasive and fearsome bona fides of diversity and inclusion provide a loophole for one side to do just that, while silencing any opposition. "We could talk about getting drunk, how we were feeling, what our club did this weekend, but the second somebody said, 'oh, there's more riots going on right now,' it was like you could hear the record scratch. Everyone's too afraid to give their opinion because they think they're going to get turned in for extremism or racial insensitivity," Devin says.

Black Lives Matter is a far-left political organization that effectively weaponizes one specific type of news story to exploit it for Democrat party votes. Not only does BLM get a pass, but support for and membership in BLM is encouraged from the Oval Office to the highest-ranking Defense Department personnel, down to the rank and file. "They just say, it's a social issue, it's a quality-of-life issue, it's not political," Devin says of BLM's hall pass. "Even though

Black Lives Matter founded it as a Marxist movement, they completely ignore that part. And if they do acknowledge it, they say, 'Well, it's still for a good cause.'"

Standing against police brutality, if there were such an epidemic, would be a good cause. The same goes for supporting fair and honest elections. But following the mass trespassing event at the U.S. Capitol on January 6, 2021, a senior officer appeared via video to address airmen at Devin's base. She had "a total Karen haircut, that distinctive short bob, and resting bitch face," Devin recalls. Officer Karen had a warning for the airmen. "If you have strong feelings, regret, or dissatisfaction with the election system, or if you think there may have been any kind of foul play, you could be showing signs of extremism," she said in the video. She went on to let service members know that if anyone was displaying unhappiness or resentment because of the election results, they could be perceived as having extremist sympathies.

"Here on the lower level, everybody gets along, we're very different. We've got Yankee-types who listen to indie rock and drink the triple IPA beers or whatever, other guys who are from the hood down in Tallahassee. But the moment we get an email from people higher up—way at the tippy top of the chain—it creates this very weird vibe," Devin says.

These emails from senior Pentagon leadership, sent throughout the entire Department of Defense, began soon after Joe Biden's inauguration. "It causes something very real in the feeling of the work environment. We'll all be sitting around having a good time and then we'll get a mass email that says, 'Hey, blacks are being discriminated against in the U.S., police are out to get you.' No statistics, no anything, no surveys. It's almost like the constant messaging more so than true evidence happening in real life. If none of this stuff have been catching the headlines in mainstream news, no one talked about this stuff before. It was fine before to make fun of a black guy listening to trap music or a white guy drinking Natty Lite and going to NASCAR races and banging his cousin. That was just common shit-talking between the guys. Once mainstream media started pushing this, it has started impacting our culture."

For Devin, Biden's Defense Department appeared to be running covert public relations for the most far-left radicals in the country, without explicitly endorsing any political activity.

"They throw out all these statements from the left, BLM, Antifa-ish sounding things, and they kind of say, 'these are what these people are fighting for, they're trying to find an answer to this question.' But they never say outright, 'we support BLM, Antifa, whatever. But they hint at it. 'Hey these guys aren't so bad, this is what their messaging is.' But they don't give that PR for the Proud Boys, or January 6th protestors. They don't say, 'these people feel like they were betrayed and lied to and disenfranchised.' No, instead they're extremists putting out false information. They're trying to dismantle our democracy. But we literally have months and months of riots and them burning down towns and cities," Devin says.

Charlie, not his real name and an active-duty senior member of the U.S. Coast Guard based near Washington, D.C., recalls a time when diversity and inclusion training in the service meant something else.

"At first, it was that we should be a melting pot, you've heard that your whole life," he told me. "Different types of people coming together with the same mission and goals. Then they started telling us, no, we're really more like a mixed salad. We want everyone to keep their identity. Someone is a cucumber and someone else is a tomato, and I thought that was really weird. Now, it's critical race theory."

After President Trump announced a ban on critical race theory in federal departments, Charlie says the Coast Guard used a surrogate in the U.S. Coast Guard Academy Alumni Association to get the message out. In February 2020, the Academy hosted a talk by diversity parasite Ibram X. Kendi where more than 1,000 members attended.

In his welcoming remarks, Rear Admiral William G. Kelly, superintendent of the academy, said the Coast Guard is committed to dismantling racism. "We know we have had our challenges, and we're constantly seeking to improve," he said, according to the school paper.

Minutes from the alumni association's meeting the following month show a speaker was invited to discuss the formation of a Racial Equity Core, where he "facilitated a conversation with the Board and staff about the book, *White Fragility*, by Robin DiAngelo. The discussion encouraged the Board and staff to reflect on their personal experiences of discussing race and racism in light of themes in the book." The speaker then "recommended that the Board consider having follow-up conversations about the book to further build on the Board's equity mindedness."

The alumni association used its magazine and other modes of correspondence to reach service members, Charlie says. "They're kind of like Hezbollah, in the sense they're a proxy, in this case to push critical race theory in the Coast Guard to the officers and cadets. When Trump banned CRT, the association could do it instead. They backdoored it."

Charlie's office is littered with Black Lives Matter paraphernalia, from signs on desks to coworkers' T-shirts and masks, and bumper stickers on the cars in the parking lot. "I grew up in the rural South, I'm used to seeing Confederate battle flags, it doesn't really shock me. I remember playing football against teams in high school with black players and their mascot was the Rebels. I know it can be used in a hateful way, but it was pretty innocuous. But we have an all-out ban on Confederate flags, even on our bumper stickers," he says.

The problem, as Charlie sees it, is consistency. "There's no doubt in my mind that January 6 was an intentional failure of security at the Capitol," he says. Charlie considered going to the Capitol that day, although leadership warned everyone against it. In the end, he didn't go. But if it had been a BLM rally, he says, officers would have been encouraged to attend and exercise their First Amendment rights. "There were times when it was all hands on deck for the Secret Service, that Antifa and BLM were going to attempt to breach the White House and if they didn't have the security in place, they would have."

"As a military officer the best thing you can do is be consistent and hold everyone to the same standards. But with January 6, now they're blaming one side, instead of saying, 'These are our fellow Americans with their own concerns.' No one said anything about the federal courthouse in Portland being invaded by Antifa."

In one training document on extremism Charlie received, the Coast Guard specifically mentioned gun shows as a hotbed of extremist activity and warned service members they may be approached by extremists at those events.

"Imagine if the NRA got a hold of that," Charlie laughed. "Yet there was nothing about what to do if you're at an Antifa rally or the Women's March and someone hands you a can of soup to throw at someone."

"I'd say they view conservatives as a liability to the service. Everyone is afraid to speak up. They don't want to get canceled from the military," he says.

"You're going to have a degradation of mission readiness and a degradation of recruits. Your majority of recruits who come from the South—you're labeling them extremists. I don't think Cape Cod liberals are signing up for the Marine Corps or the Coast Guard."

On the day of the stand down for the Department of Defense, Devin from the Air Force walked into class to find one of his favorite commanders at the helm—a political science guy, well read, with a deep understanding of geopolitics and the role of the nation state. Airmen were seated six feet apart, masked up, and the commander initiated the extremism training with an item the Pentagon had not included in the syllabus. Underneath each seat, the commander had placed a booklet containing copies of the U.S. Constitution and the Declaration of Independence. He read them to the class.

Servicemembers take an oath to defend America against all enemies foreign and domestic, "But he didn't emphasize 'and domestic' the way all the politicians do now," Devin recalls. "He said we have to follow the lawful orders that come from above and that's why we are here right now, and I felt like that was a dig. He said he didn't believe anyone here was an extremist."

By the end of the presentation, Devin was left with the impression that anyone who supports President Trump or is sympathetic to the Proud Boys or similar groups qualified to be turned in for extremism.

"They described the Proud Boys as basically the Taliban. They'll reach out to you, they target the downtrodden, they hope you'll blame all your problems on black and brown people—and this is coming from the Pentagon."

The signs of extremism were sweeping and nebulous. "It was like looking at the symptoms of COVID. They'll show you twenty things and you're like, well, I have at least one of them, I guess I have COVID."

"I hate to say it, but, yeah, it's women. Women are always the ones who bring this stuff up," Devin said about DEI issues on the job. Shortly after we spoke, the Air Force announced it would begin issuing pregnancy flight suits. With growing international threats from Russia and China on the horizon, military preparedness seemed to be taking a backseat to DEI warm fuzzies under the Biden administration. Rank and file began to wonder if, aside from sinking workplace morale, these efforts would turn away the exact type of men you'd want enlisting to defend your country.

Appearing on Fox News in December 2021 to discuss the pregnancy flight suits, commentator and Marine Corps combat veteran Jesse Kelly summed it up. "China right now, and Russia, they're both testing hypersonic missiles that can turn New York City to ash. Russia is actually developing and has developed satellites that can push our satellites out of orbit and cripple our military. Our military, though, they're focused on the important things. We want to focus on climate change, and we definitely have to make sure there are enough tampons in the restrooms at the Pentagon," he said.

"We don't need a military that's woman-friendly. We don't need a military that's gay-friendly, with all due respect to the Air Force. We need a military that's flat-out hostile. We need a military full of Type-A men who want to sit on a throne of Chinese skulls, but we don't have that now."

Chapter Six

So You've Been Sent to Diversity Training: How to Get Through It Without Losing Your Mind, Your Job, or Your Sense of Humor

Over lunch the other day a friend who works for a major media conglomerate told me about a teleconference with hundreds of coworkers across the country. His company recently merged with another large media organization, it was national news, and workers convened for a briefing on what to expect.

When the leaders opened the conference for questions, the first hand to go up belonged to a young, white woman. "What's the company's plan for DEI," she asked. My friend was beside himself. *Really? That's your question,* he wondered. "It's like a religion for these people," he said. "It's no different than if a fundamentalist Christian had stood up and said, 'How will this merger help us spread the message of Jesus Christ.'"

How did we get here, he contemplated. Was media saturation to blame? Perhaps it's generational. As Millennials come to dominate the workforce, this crop's desperate need to fancy themselves liberators and freedom fighters—storming the beaches at Normandy or marching in Selma with each trending hashtag and TikTok dance routine, on an endless moral crusade against imaginary monsters and in the service of magical victims—can't be entirely the product of luxury and omphaloskepsis. Their parents' generation sold out their country and rigged the system. When the Boomers shepherded their kids into crippling student loan debt, chasing art and idealism on campus as they had—or wish they had—Millennials were slapped with harsh realities when they emerged from college. They didn't realize they'd never own a home, at least not anytime soon. That strong men and fathers mattered. That the alternative to a society built on marriage, fidelity, and the family might be one where your office becomes your home and the government your daddy. Increasingly, and ushered in by the COVID-19 lockdowns, your home also has become your office. Work goes with you everywhere on the phone in your pocket, and everything makes its way into work.

This symbiosis of home, society, and the office spread to work culture across the economy. It's what Millennials want, it makes them more productive, companies were told. Compare that to the place you sleep—a grim, overpriced pod in the Mission District that greets you with mountains of laundry and Trader Joe's wine, with little to keep you company other than a smelly cat and the Internet. If that's your life, who'd want to leave campus?

Then you've been inundated for decades by a script, one perpetuated because it makes money and awards power, that the nation in which you live is unfair, racist, and terrible to the core. It would seem strange, given the porous boundaries of home-work-society, if such issues weren't repeatedly addressed on the clock. Your corporation is not a place where you earn a paycheck. It, like you, is a global citizen. It is not only your world but *the* world.

Companies today rarely have employees, instead they're called teammates, partners, and family members. Silicon

Valley, the world's most powerful industry, one created for and by Millennials, doesn't have offices. They have campuses, tending to every need of their employees. There are food courts, gyms, game rooms, floating chairs and bean bag chairs, free cooking classes, shuttles to drive you to and from work, ball pits, mini golf courses, massage parlors, CEOs in pajamas, and an open-door policy on bringing your pet to work. And that's just at Google.

And yet, something seems off. Are all white people evil? Do I owe my existence to transgender women of color? Is there really a problem in this country, or at this company, with bigotry? Is any of this necessary?

Challenging your diversity czar might not get you fired, but it will cause plenty of headaches. Speaking up means you may attract the scorn of any Saviors and Parasites, whose worldview is unchangeable, lurking down the hall. Parasites and Saviors love to get people fired and canceled, and they're always up for the task. Keep in mind that normal people suffer these trainings just like you, by staring at the clock, sending emails, or writing their grocery lists.

If you find yourself in a particularly aggressive and hateful diversity seminar, taking your concerns through the proper, official company channels may be fruitless. Once you start ruffling feathers in Big Diversity, you can start the clock on your exit from the company. It raises eyebrows and makes people queasy. No company can afford to be perceived as antimedley and subtractive, no matter how much sense your arguments make. The Sandia Labs whistleblower thought he'd teach his own course at the company to expose the belittling and obnoxious take on race relations that had been spoon-fed to workers.

"I offered to host a class correcting the record," he said on YouTube. "I was told that the company is not hosting a forum for debate and to keep my opinions at home and to get back to work. I was told by the senior manager of HR that, quote, 'It is not our job to fact check the materials for accuracy' and they refused to pull down the offending materials."

It's not just about fact checking. Most materials presented as part of your company's diversity curriculum probably haven't undergone any sort of review. It would take balls visible from orbit to tell a diversity czar that they're spreading lies. Peterson from Sandia Labs decided to take steps to correct the record anyway. If he couldn't host his own class, then he'd ask to have the offending materials removed from the company's website. A weeks-long runaround through various offices and levels of leadership followed—from level one management to level two, to Human Resources, to ethics and government relations offices, back to management, and back to HR only finally to be told, "You are free to have your own opinions at home and essentially the matter is closed."

"This is my advice to all those listening now, and I want to quote directly from our [Diversity and Inclusion] Town Hall," Peterson concludes in his video. "It can be easy to find resources that reinforce feelings or beliefs that we already have. As you're researching just be cognizant of who you are reading and why they were writing it. Think about confirmation bias. Are you looking to answer the questions that you already believe you know the answer to or are you actually seeking out different perspectives and thinking about learning from an inclusive standpoint?"

Imagine you're in East Berlin on November 9, 1989, watching neighbors cascade into the West as the wall comes down panel by panel. Hours earlier, you may have had an encounter with some of these same people. In casual conversation they commended the Soviet government, spat upon the West, repeated verbatim lines you'd read in the government newspapers. But now they're taking up pick-axes against the concrete barrier, celebrating in the street, pouring champagne, and lining up at McDonald's on the other side of the crumbling divide.

A week earlier, Soviet leader Mikhail Gorbachev met with the then-leader of East Germany, Egon Krenz, to discuss easing restrictions on border crossings. "Our mutual thinking with Krenz at the meeting had been that the question of German reunification was 'still not relevant,' 'not really on the agenda,' and that is where we were coming from," Gorbachev wrote in his memoir. After that meeting, in a speech, a member of the politburo quietly declared the border open.

According to one published account from a KGB officer in East Berlin, "It was a regular announcement, nothing out of the ordinary. I did not foresee the speech arousing any sort of major reaction at all." Instead, East Germans wasted no time and flooded to the border in anticipation of reunification and freedom.

You thought the wall would stand forever. The funny realization comes over you—it was all an act. No telling how long your comrades privately felt the same as you. The economist Timur Kuran called this phenomenon preference falsification—communicating a preference that differs from one's own true feelings.

Misrepresenting one's preferences occurs under perceived social pressures. The public frequently does this when speaking to pollsters, journalists, researchers, or each other if they believe the conveyed opinion is more socially acceptable than what they really believe. We do this all the time—when asked by your friend how you feel about her deadbeat boyfriend, or if you complimented your aunt's food but found it to be dry and overspiced. Preference falsification also has societywide implications. "Preference falsification shapes collective decisions, orients structural change, sustains social stability, distorts human knowledge, and conceals political possibilities," according to Harvard University Press.

Most people understand, if privately, that the outsized focus on race in twenty-first century America is a grift and a scam. Normal people are concerned with the price of gasoline, saving for college, or what to make for dinner. They understand Americans are welcoming and good-natured. That we live in the most diverse nation on Earth and no one needs to be belittled and nannied about how to navigate it. Despite certain forces, acting for profit or power, convincing you otherwise, nothing you'll learn in your diversity courses applies to you; it is OK to reject it. Doing so may save your company. Diversity of thought and perspective gave rise to the greatest nation in the world and built all its most innovative companies. Any organization with a rigid ideological system in place is doomed to failure.

In the private sector, take Kodak, for example. Each day over 1.8 billion photographs are uploaded on the Internet. For most of the 20th century Kodak was synonymous with picture-taking—we even called a photograph a "Kodak moment"—but the company filed for Chapter 11 in 2012. Today, no one is quite sure what Kodak does anymore. Or there's Sears, the ghost of a department store still occasionally found anchoring windswept shopping malls on the bad side of town. Sears invented mail-order shopping. It should have become Amazon but didn't get anywhere close. Business analysts sometimes cite those two companies as examples of how one-directional leadership, rigidity, and a culture of fear hindered innovation and led to disaster.

Same goes for governments. The Soviet Union was once said to be the world's most highly educated society of in-the-box thinkers. Ask any Sovietologist what led to the sudden collapse and they'll tell you there was no system in place to cope with reforms toward liberalism brought in by Gorbachev. Anything but communist philosophy had been banned for decades. The one-directional structure of the society meant everyone lived in fear of speaking truth to the person above them.

"It's normal that most people could not predict that the Soviet Union, one of the two global superpowers, would fall apart. Such events are very rare in history. However, there were signs. If something cannot go on forever, it will stop—that's [American economist] Herbert Stein's law, formulated in 1986, and not about the Soviet Union. The Soviet economy could not generate productivity growth. Gorbachev had to borrow to provide stable living standards. The Soviet Union could not reform as the system was rigid," economist Sergei Guriev told *Bloomberg News* in 2021, on the thirtieth anniversary of the fall.

Silicon Valley, once synonymous with innovation, is heading in that direction and taking the rest of society along with it. Social media's entire business is speech and expression. Yet, in a few short years, they're preoccupied with censorship and curtailment. It's suicide, but no one seems to mind. Few inside will speak up. Like many work environments, petty tyrants score power through emotional bullying and bowdlerization while leadership aligns itself with the destructive, globalist wing of the Democratic party, which is also a big fan of shutting people up and taking away their dignity.

Not everyone can be Dave Chappelle. In October 2021, Netflix employees staged a walkout from the company's Hollywood headquarters and joined demonstrators outside to protest the megastar's comedy special, "The Closer," streaming on the platform. According to one activist named Neverending Nina, interviewed by KTLA, Chappelle's comedy was guilty of "censoring the trauma of trans people," whatever that means. In fact, in the wildly successful special, he was one of the few comedians unafraid to mock aspects of trans culture. Calls to boycott the network and employees threatening to quit continued for months. In May, the company finally came out with an official response to the hubbub: if you're offended by the content the company is producing, you can quit. "Depending on your role, you may need to work on titles you perceive to be harmful," a memo to employees read. "If you'd find it hard to support our content breadth, Netflix may not be the best place for you." Earlier in the year, the streaming giant signed a deal with Chappelle to produce four more specials.

As George Orwell once wrote, "The real division is not between conservatives and revolutionaries but between authoritarians and libertarians." DEI theology is contrary to both nature and common sense. Now that this has come to nearly all workplaces, the only socially acceptable option is to agree. It's a status quo maintained by fear and passivity; one that might destroy your life if you step out of line. Fear of running up against the mob keeps people in check. But what if the mob is an illusion? The tens of thousands of unafraid, cheerful audience members seated for a Dave Chappelle Netflix taping—not to mention the millions viewing at home—dwarf the hundred or so protestors outside Netflix. What if the pitchfork-wielders are fewer and less frightening than you've been led to believe?

The more people stand up and say no, the more the hollowness of this ideologically totalitarian movement is exposed, and sooner or later it will have to be defeated. But uprooting it from American institutions will not be easy. There is no magic wand to make all of this disappear; DEI bureaucrats are very well ensconced. Think of yourself as part of that silent majority in the former Soviet Union. Everyday people are resisting in ways that are not dangerous to their well-being and livelihood. As we saw with the former Soviet leadership, the emperor had no clothes. A cascade is coming.

Over that lunch the other day, when my friend described the corporate merger meeting, he couldn't shake this odd sense about the woman who rushed to ask, in front of the whole company, about diversity and inclusion. He thought for a moment about what plagued him concerning her eagerness to get on the record. "The whole thing just seemed so," he paused and searched the room for the right word then scooped up some guacamole on a chip. "I don't know. Fake."

Acknowledgments

When Adam Bellow from Bombardier Books phoned me up with the idea to write a book on workplace DEI training, I jumped on it, cognizant of how often the queer and sinister lurks in the seemingly mundane. This book would not have been possible without Adam's keen eye and guidance. It also would not have been possible without the dedication of my research assistant, Mitchell Sances—an intelligent, reliable, and hardworking young writer, with a bright career ahead of him.

Since my abrupt exit from mainstream media several years ago, I'll be forever grateful to Freddy Gray, Matt McDonald, and Zack Christenson at *The Spectator*, who gave me the perfect home to vent, brood, and laugh on the page. And an especially big thank you to Monica Crowley who facilitated that relationship.

Richard Grenell and Charles Moran—two fearless leaders who fight everyday for their country and their tribe—took a chance on me when I needed it the most and for that, I will always be thankful.

I would have lost my sanity and resolve long ago if not for my friends: Alex, who's always there when I need to get out of the house, or out of my head, to slam oysters and Micheladas; Nicky, who makes me laugh until my sides hurt; Peter, for his warmth and sass; Jonathan, for his love of history and tradition; and Ward and Paul, who always make you feel so at home.

When you're in the grimy world of political journalism it helps to have a loving family around you, even if you don't always agree on everything. I'm blessed to have the support of my mother, Martha; stepfather, Ron; father, Gary; his girlfriend, Pam; my sister, Holly, and niece, Mia.

And, lastly, for Nate. You changed my life and I'm a better man for having known you. You inspire me every day to strive and succeed. You believe in me more than I could ever believe in myself. I love you.

About the Author

Chadwick Moore is a public speaker, TV commentator, columnist, and contributing editor at *The Spectator*. He's the former editor-at-large for *Out* and *The Advocate* and former writer for the *New York Times* and *Playboy*, before he was canceled in 2017 for coming out as a conservative. A native of Tennessee, he lives in Brooklyn, New York.